REVISE AQA GCSE (9–1)
Physics
REVISION GUIDE
Foundation

Series Consultant: Harry Smith

Author: Dr Mike O'Neill

Also available to support your revision:

Revise GCSE Study Skills Guide   9781292318875

The **Revise GCSE Study Skills Guide** is full of tried-and-trusted hints and tips for how to learn more effectively. It gives you techniques to help you achieve your best – throughout your GCSE studies and beyond!

Revise GCSE Revision Planner   9781292318868

The **Revise GCSE Revision Planner** helps you to plan and organise your time, step-by-step, throughout your GCSE revision. Use this book and wall chart to mastermind your revision.

For the full range of Pearson revision titles across KS2, 11+, KS3, GCSE, Functional Skills, AS/A Level and BTEC visit:
www.pearsonschools.co.uk/revise

Question difficulty
Look at this scale next to each exam-style question. It tells you how difficult the question is.

Contents

1-to-1 page match with the Physics Foundation Revision Workbook ISBN 9781292131474

A small bit of small print:

AQA publishes Sample Assessment Material and the Specification on its website. This is the official content and this book should be used in conjunction with it. The questions in *Now try this* have been written to help you practise every topic in the book. Remember: the real exam questions may not look like this.

Energy stores and systems

A system is an object or a group of objects. There are changes in the way energy is stored when a system changes.

Examples of energy stores

There are eight main energy stores.

Energy store	Example
chemical	fuel, food, battery
kinetic	moving objects
gravitational potential	raised mass
elastic	stretched spring
thermal	hot object
magnetic	two magnets
electrostatic	two charges
nuclear	nuclear fuel

Conservation of energy

Energy can be transferred usefully to other stores and it can be wasted or dissipated to the surroundings. However, energy cannot be created or destroyed – the total energy in a closed system is the same after as it was before the transfer.

A closed system is an isolated system where no energy flows in or out of the system.

Examples of energy transfers

1 When an object is thrown upwards, the kinetic energy store decreases and the gravitational potential energy store increases.

2 When a moving object hits an obstacle, kinetic energy can be transferred and energy can be dissipated as thermal energy.

3 The kinetic energy store of an object will increase when it is accelerated by a force.

4 When a vehicle brakes, the kinetic energy store decreases and the thermal energy store increases due to friction in the brakes.

5 When a kettle boils, energy is transferred electrically to increase the thermal store in the water.

Energy transfers

Energy can be transferred in three ways:
- by **heating**
- through the use of **forces**
- electrically by an **electric current**.

Energy transfers can be shown by flow diagrams. The flow diagram shows the changes in energy stores and the transfers for a falling object:

transfer by force of gravity → transfer by: – heating – sound waves

gravitational potential energy store → kinetic energy store → energy store of the surroundings

In all the examples, energy will be transferred to less useful forms, or wasted. It is dissipated to the thermal energy store of the surroundings.

Worked example

The batteries in a battery-operated fan contain a total of 100 J of energy.

Draw a flow diagram to show the changes in the energy stores and the transfers that are taking place.

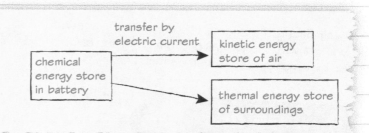

transfer by electric current

chemical energy store in battery → kinetic energy store of air

chemical energy store in battery → thermal energy store of surroundings

Now try this

1 Draw an energy store flow diagram for a car driving up a hill.　**(4 marks)**

2 Describe the changes in energy stores and the energy transfers for a swinging pendulum.
　(4 marks)

1

Changes in energy

Energy changes can be calculated for a moving object, a stretched spring and an object raised above the ground.

Maths skills — Kinetic energy

Kinetic energy is stored in moving objects and is calculated using the equation:

$$\text{kinetic energy in J} = \frac{1}{2} \times \text{mass in kg} \times \text{(speed) in (m/s)}^2$$

$$E_k = \frac{1}{2} m v^2$$

LEARN IT!
IT'S NOT ON THE EQUATIONS LIST

Kinetic energy is directly proportional to the mass of the moving object: doubling the mass doubles the kinetic energy of the moving object.

It is directly proportional to the square of the speed, so doubling the speed means that the E_k increases by a factor of four.

The amount of gravitational potential energy gained by an object raised above the ground is calculated using the equation:

$$\text{gravitational potential energy in J} = \text{mass in kg} \times \text{gravitational field strength in N/kg} \times \text{height in m}$$

$$E_p = m g h$$

LEARN IT!
IT'S NOT ON THE EQUATIONS LIST

The amount of elastic potential energy stored in a stretched spring is calculated using the equation:

$$\text{elastic potential energy in J} = \frac{1}{2} \times \text{spring constant in N/m} \times \text{(extension) in m}^2$$

$$E_e = \frac{1}{2} k e^2$$

When calculating the energy stored in joules, ensure that you convert the extension from centimetres to metres by dividing the value in centimetres by 100.

Remember to square the value of speed when calculating the kinetic energy. The term v^2 means $v \times v$.

Worked example

 (a) A mass of 800 g is moving at 14 m/s. Calculate its kinetic energy. **(3 marks)**

$E_k = \frac{1}{2} m v^2$

$E_k = \frac{1}{2} \times 0.8 \times 14^2 = 78.4 \text{ J}$

 (b) A body of mass 4.8 kg has kinetic energy of 200 J. Calculate the speed it is moving at. **(4 marks)**

$200 \text{ J} = \frac{1}{2} \times 4.8 \times v^2$

Rearranging gives $v = \sqrt{400 \div 4.8} = 9.1 \text{ m/s}$

Worked example

A body of mass 73 kg is lifted through a vertical height of 26 m. Calculate how much gravitational potential energy it has gained. **(3 marks)**

$E_p = m g h$

$= 73 \text{ kg} \times 10 \text{ N/kg} \times 26 \text{ m} = 18980 \text{ J}$

Worked example

A spring is distorted elastically. It increases its length by 25 cm when a total weight of 12 N is added. Calculate the total energy stored in the spring. **(4 marks)**

energy stored = work done

$E_e = \frac{1}{2} k e^2$

$= \frac{1}{2} \times 48 \text{ N/m} \times (0.25 \text{ m})^2 = 1.5 \text{ J}$

Now try this

1 Calculate the kinetic energy store of a ball of mass 12 kg moving at a speed of 8 m/s. **(3 marks)**
2 Calculate how much gravitational potential energy has been gained by a 25 kg mass that has been raised through a height of 36 m. **(3 marks)**
3 Calculate the increase in the elastic potential energy store of a spring of spring constant 50 N/m when it is extended by 35 cm. **(3 marks)**

Energy changes in systems

You can calculate the amount of energy stored in or released from a system as its temperature changes. In order to do this, you need to know the specific heat capacity of the material in the system.

Specific heat capacity

Specific heat capacity is the **thermal energy** that must be **transferred** to change the **temperature** of **1 kg** of a material **by 1 °C**. Different materials have different specific heat capacities. Water has a value of 4200 J/kg°C, which means that 1 kg of water needs 4200 J of thermal energy to be transferred to raise its temperature by 1 °C.

You can calculate the thermal energy required using the equation: $\Delta E = m\,c\,\Delta\theta$

$$\text{change in thermal energy in J} = \text{mass in kg} \times \text{specific heat capacity in J/kg°C} \times \text{change in temperature in °C}$$

Typical specific heat capacities

Typical values are given in the table.

Material	Specific heat capacity in J/kg °C
air	1005
water	4200
aluminium	900
concrete	880

Finding specific heat capacity

You can use this apparatus to find the specific heat capacity of a metal block.

An insulating jacket is placed around the metal block to reduce the amount of wasted energy transferred to the thermal store of the surroundings.

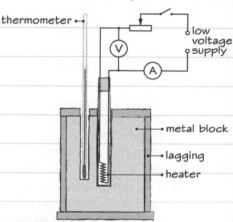

Worked example

A mass of 800 g has a specific heat capacity of 900 J/kg °C and is heated from 20 °C to 80 °C. Calculate how much thermal energy was supplied. **(3 marks)**

$\Delta E = m\,c\,\Delta\theta$

$0.8 \times 900 \times (80 - 20) = 43\,200\,\text{J}$

It requires 3151 J of energy to raise the temperature of 1 kg of this metal block by 1 °C.

Worked example

A total of 300 000 J of electrical energy is required to raise the temperature of a metal block of mass 2.8 kg from 18 °C to 52 °C. Calculate the specific heat capacity of the metal block. **(4 marks)**

$\Delta E = m\,c\,\Delta\theta$

$300\,000\,\text{J} = 2.8\,\text{kg} \times c \times (52\,°C - 18\,°C)$

$c = 300\,000\,\text{J} \div (2.8\,\text{kg} \times 34\,°C)$

$= 3151\,\text{J/kg}\,°C$

Now try this

1 Define the term specific heat capacity. **(3 marks)**

2 Calculate the energy required to raise the temperature of 15 kg of water from 18 °C to 74 °C. **(3 marks)**

3 A metal block of mass 1.25 kg is connected to a heater which transfers 32 256 J of energy to the block. The temperature of the metal block increases by 26 °C. Calculate its specific heat capacity. **(4 marks)**

Specific heat capacity

Practical skills You can determine the specific heat capacity of water using an electric heater.

Required practical

Aim

to determine the specific heat capacity of water and to describe the behaviour of ice when melting

Apparatus

water, thermometer, electric heater, power supply, insulation, beaker, electronic balance

Method

1 Set the apparatus up as shown in the diagram.

2 Measure the mass (m) of the water using an electronic balance.

3 Record the potential difference (V) of the power supply and the current (I) through the heater.

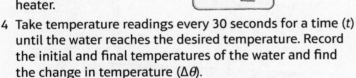

thermometer

to power supply

electric heater

4 Take temperature readings every 30 seconds for a time (t) until the water reaches the desired temperature. Record the initial and final temperatures of the water and find the change in temperature ($\Delta\theta$).

Results

Plot a graph of temperature against time. Calculate the specific heat capacity. The value c is found by substituting the results into the equation $c = (V I t) \div (m \Delta\theta)$.

Conclusion

The specific heat capacity of water is the energy required to change 1 kg of water by a temperature of 1 °C. Its value is about 4200 J/kg °C.

There is more information about specific heat capacity on page 3, and more information about the energy transferred by a known current and potential difference on page 22.

Having insulation around the beaker will transfer less energy to the surroundings and give a more accurate value for the specific heat capacity of the water.

When recording the temperature readings, avoid parallax errors by reading the thermometer scale at eye level. Record the temperature values regularly, at equal intervals and ensure that the thermometer is in the middle of the liquid.

You can explore the behaviour of melting ice by drawing a graph like the one shown below. When ice melts, it changes state, but its temperature does not change.

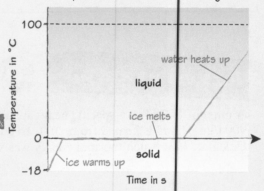

The word 'specific' in this context is for 1 kg of mass. In other words, the values for specific heat capacity and latent heat are for when 1 kg either changes temperature by 1 °C or when it changes state.

Now try this

1 Explain why insulating the beaker leads to a more accurate value for the specific heat capacity of water. **(3 marks)**

2 Explain how the graph above would change for heating the same mass of aluminium that has a specific heat capacity of 880 J/kg °C. **(2 marks)**

3 The results of an experiment to determine the specific heat capacity of 0.5 kg of a liquid are as follows. A heater transferred 28 800 J of energy to the liquid. The temperature of the liquid increased from 20 °C to 50 °C. Work out the specific heat capacity of the liquid.

(3 marks)

Power

Power is defined as the rate at which energy is transferred or work is done. The greater the power rating of a device, the more energy it transfers each second.

Power

Power is the rate of doing work (how fast energy is transferred). Power is measured in **watts (W)**. 1 watt is 1 joule of energy being transferred every second.

$$\text{power in W} = \frac{\text{energy transferred in J}}{\text{time in s}}, \quad P = \frac{E}{t}$$

$$\text{power in W} = \frac{\text{work done in J}}{\text{time taken in s}}, \quad P = \frac{W}{t}$$

 **LEARN IT!** IT'S NOT ON THE EQUATIONS LIST

E / $P \times t$

Typical power ratings of devices

Device	Power rating in W
hairdryer	1500
TV	50
microwave oven	850
jet engine	8.2×10^7

A typical nuclear power station generates 1 GW. (1 GW = 1×10^9 W)

A hairdryer with a power of 1800 W transfers 1800 J each second.

Energy transferred and work done

The calculation for the work done or energy transferred depends on the nature of the energy transfer that has taken place.

For a change in gravitational potential energy, use the equation $E_p = m\,g\,h$

For work done by a force, use the equation $W = F\,s$

For electrical energy changes, use the equations $E = Q\,V$ and $Q = I\,t$

Worked example

(a) A microwave oven transfers 48 000 J of energy in 1 minute. Calculate the power rating of the microwave oven. **(3 marks)**

power = energy transferred ÷ time

= 48 000 J ÷ 60 s

= 800 W (or 800 J/s)

(b) A force of 120 N moves an object 40 m in 2 minutes. Calculate the power. **(4 marks)**

work done = force × distance in m

= 120 N × 40 m = 4800 J

power = work done ÷ time

= 4800 J ÷ 120 s = 40 W (or 40 J/s)

Worked example

A climber of mass 78 kg scales a wall of height 30 m in 5 minutes. Work out the power the climber uses to scale the wall. Use $g = 10$ N/kg. **(3 marks)**

energy transferred = $m\,g\,h$

= 78 kg × 10 N/kg × 30 m

= 23 400 J

power (W) = energy transferred (J) ÷ time taken (s)

= 23 400 J ÷ 300 s = 78 W (or 78 J/s)

Remember to convert from minutes to seconds when calculating power in watts.

Now try this

1 Two identical garage doors use different electric motors to lift the door through the same height. One motor opens the door in 6 seconds. The other opens the door in 8 seconds. Compare the powers of the motors. **(3 marks)**

2 Calculate how much energy an 1800 W hairdryer transfers when used for 8 minutes. **(3 marks)**

3 Calculate the power of a light bulb that transfers 3600 J of energy in 1 minute. **(3 marks)**

Energy transfers and efficiency

The rate at which a material transfers thermal energy depends on a number of factors. The **efficiency** of a device is a measure of how much **useful** energy it transfers.

Thermal energy transfer

The rate at which thermal energy is transferred through a wall of a house depends on:

1. the difference in temperature between the warmer interior and the colder exterior
2. the thickness of the walls
3. the thermal conductivity of the walls.

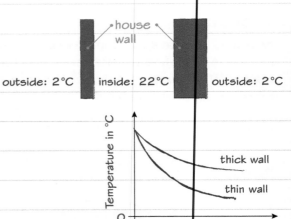

house wall

outside: 2°C | inside: 22°C | outside: 2°C

thick wall
thin wall

Temperature in °C — Time in s

Efficiency

All machines **waste** some of the **energy** they **transfer**. Most machines waste energy as **heat** energy. The **efficiency** of a machine is a way of saying how good it is at transferring energy into **useful** forms.

A very efficient machine has an efficiency that is nearly 100%. The higher the efficiency, the better the machine is at transferring energy to useful forms.

You can reduce unwanted energy transfers, for example through lubrication to reduce friction, using wires with low resistance in electrical circuits, and streamlining shapes for moving objects to reduce air resistance.

Thermal conductivity

A material with a high thermal conductivity is a better conductor of energy than one with a lower thermal conductivity. The rate at which the blue wall transfers energy is greater than that of the red wall.

outside: 2°C | inside: 22°C

house walls made of different materials

outside: 2°C | inside: 22°C

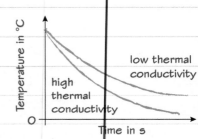

low thermal conductivity
high thermal conductivity

Temperature in °C — Time in s

Worked example

A motor transfers 100 J of energy by electricity: 60 J are transferred as kinetic energy, 12 J as sound energy and 28 J as thermal energy. Calculate the efficiency of the motor. **(3 marks)**

$$\text{efficiency} = \frac{\text{useful energy transferred by the machine}}{\text{total energy supplied to the machine}} \times 100\%$$

total useful energy = 60 J

$$\text{efficiency} = \frac{60\ J}{100\ J} \times 100\%$$

$$= 60\% \text{ (or 0.6 as a decimal)}$$

LEARN IT!
IT'S NOT ON THE EQUATIONS LIST

← Efficiency does not have units.

← No machine is ever 100% efficient. If you calculate an efficiency greater than 100% you have done something wrong!

Now try this

1. A device transfers 14 J out of every 20 J supplied to useful energy stores. Calculate the efficiency of the device. **(2 marks)**
2. Explain why it is not possible for any device to be 100% efficient. **(3 marks)**

Use an electric appliance such as a kettle as an example.

Thermal insulation

Practical skills You can investigate how different materials affect the rate of cooling of a material and how the thickness of a material affects the rate of cooling.

Required practical

> Insulating materials could include: newspaper, corrugated cardboard, bubble wrap, sawdust and polystyrene granules.

Investigating thermal insulation

Aim

to measure the rate of cooling of a beaker of hot water when insulated with different materials and with different thicknesses of the same material

> Be careful not to burn or scald yourself with hot water or steam from the kettle.

Apparatus

beakers, thermometers, kettle and water, pieces of cardboard, scissors, stopwatch, insulating materials and different amounts of one insulating material

Method 1: investigating thickness

1 Wrap three beakers in different thicknesses of the same insulating material.
2 Put the same amount of hot water into each beaker. Use a piece of cardboard for a lid with a hole for the thermometer.
3 Record the temperature of the water every 3 minutes for 20 minutes.

> The **dependent variable** in this investigation is the temperature of the water and the **independent variable** is the thickness of the insulating material.
>
> The dependent variable is plotted on the y-axis and the independent variable on the x-axis.

Method 2: investigating different materials

Place some insulating material around the inside of a beaker. Place a smaller beaker inside the insulation. Pour hot water into the smaller beaker.

Then follow method 1 from step 2 onwards. Repeat with a different insulating material.

> So that the results are accurate, valid and reliable, try to ensure that the same **mass** of insulating material is used for each of the insulating materials.

Results

Record your results in a table similar to this one. Plot a graph of temperature of the water against time.

Method 1				
Number of layers of insulation	Temperature in °C			
	at start	after 3 minutes	after 6 minutes	after 9 minutes
0	80	73	67	62
1	80	74	69	65
2	80	75	71	68
Method 2				
Material				
no insulation	80	73	67	62
bubble wrap	80	76	72	70
newspaper	80	75	71	68

Conclusion

The greater the thickness of insulating material, the slower the rate at which the hot water cools.

The lower the thermal conductivity of the insulating material, the lower the rate at which the hot water cools.

Now try this

1 Describe **three** potential sources of error that may arise in this investigation. **(3 marks)**
2 Explain why there are data for 'no insulation' in the table of results for method 2. **(2 marks)**
3 Explain why the mass of each insulating material should be kept the same in method 2 for all the materials. **(4 marks)**

Energy resources

Renewable and non-renewable resources are used for transport, heating and electricity generation. Renewable energy resources can be replenished as they are being used and will not run out. Non-renewable energy resources cannot be replaced and will eventually run out.

Resource	Description, uses and issues
biomass	Taken from living or recently living organisms including methane gas from animal waste and sewage. Used for fuels such as methanol in transport and as fuel in power stations. Carbon neutral: carbon dioxide released when burnt is the same amount that the organism took in when living.
wind	Wind turbines transfer the kinetic energy of the wind to electrical energy by turning a generator. Do not work if not windy or too much wind.
hydroelectricity	Water stored in a reservoir is used to generate electrical energy when it flows downhill through a generator. Generally reliable but will not be used if the reservoir runs dry in a drought.
geothermal energy	Thermal energy released from radioactive decay within the Earth heats surrounding rocks. Water is pumped down to be heated by the rocks. The resulting hot water or steam is used to heat homes or turn generators to generate electrical energy. Reliable due to constant heat supply.
tidal power	Kinetic energy of tidal streams or from sea water flowing through barrages used by turbines to generate electricity. Tidal power is available at predictable times, but not all of the time. There are few places where these can be situated and they may affect wildlife habitats.
solar power	Solar panels use radiation from the Sun to heat water for use in homes or to generate electricity. Solar cells generate electricity. Can be used to supply energy to people in remote areas. Does not work when not sunny.
water waves	Water waves turn a generator to generate electricity. Unreliable due to small or no wave motion on calm days.
fossil fuels	Coal, oil and gas are burned in power stations to heat water, which becomes steam and turns turbines to generate electricity. Fuels such as petrol, kerosene, diesel and oil are used in transport and heating homes. Reliable, but produce carbon dioxide which leads to global warming.
nuclear	Uranium or plutonium release energy from the fission of their nuclei. The energy released is used in power stations to generate electricity. Reliable. Produces around 10 000 times more energy per kilogram compared with fossil fuels, but also produces large amounts of dangerous radioactive waste.

Worked example

Explain why environmental problems are not always solved by science. **(3 marks)**

Science can identify environmental issues like global warming, but political, social, ethical and economic factors may not allow these to be addressed. There may be resistance from people not wanting wind turbines near their homes or animal habitats to be destroyed, and there may be financial constraints, so politicians don't allow resources to be built due to cost or other social, political or ethical issues.

Now try this

 1 Describe how the different renewable and non-renewable resources are used for transport. **(4 marks)**

 2 Compare the advantages and disadvantages of solar power and nuclear energy. **(4 marks)**

Patterns of energy use

The patterns and trends in how humans have used energy resources have changed over time.

Patterns and trends in energy use

The use of energy resources has changed over the years. This is because of several factors:

1 **the world's population** In the past 200 years, the population of the world has risen from 1 billion to 7 billion people.

2 **the development of technology** Vehicles such as cars, trains and planes and other devices have increased in number and these all require energy.

3 **electrical energy** Power stations require fuels in order to generate electricity.

Growth in world population

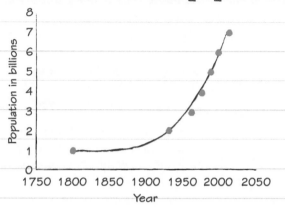

Trends in the world's energy use

As the graph shows, most of the world's energy use has been fossil fuels. Before about 1900, biomass in the form of wood was the major source of fuel and its use has remained constant over time.

In more recent years, there has been an increase in the use of nuclear fuel and hydroelectric power.

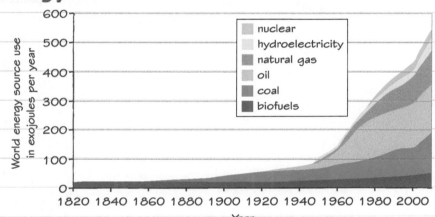

Worked example

Compare the shape of the world's population graph with that of the energy use graph. **(4 marks)**

They are similar in that, as the population increases, the total energy used will increase. They differ in that the total energy use has increased faster than the population. As societies develop, they use more technology that requires energy to run it. This means that the average amount of energy used per person also increases.

The future?

It is not possible to continue using the Earth's non-renewable energy reserves to the extent that they are being used now. They are a finite reserve, so will run out and not be replaced.

Greater use of fossil fuels will lead to more carbon dioxide in the atmosphere. There will be greater global warming, leading to severe weather, flooding and threats to food supplies.

Now try this

1 Describe the main issues with using the Earth's energy supplies. **(2 marks)**

2 Wood is a biofuel. Suggest why wood has been used constantly for many years, whereas other fuels have only been used much more recently. **(3 marks)**

Extended response – Energy

There will be at least one 6-mark question on your exam paper. For these questions, you will need to think scientifically and structure your answer logically, showing how the points you make are related to each other. You can revise the topics for this question, which is about **the principle of the conservation of energy**, on page 1.

Worked example

Figure 1 shows the arrangement of apparatus for a simple pendulum. Figure 2 shows how the kinetic energy of the pendulum changes with time.

Describe the energy transfers taking place during the motion of the simple pendulum. Your answer should refer to the energy stores and energy transfers that are involved.

(6 marks)

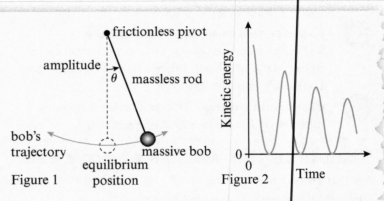

Figure 1

Figure 2

Initially, the pendulum has to be raised through a small angle, so it will gain gravitational potential energy. Once released, this gravitational potential energy store will be transferred mainly to a kinetic energy store, with some energy being dissipated as thermal energy in the surroundings from friction due to air resistance.

The principle of conservation of energy states that the total energy of the system at any time must be the same, since energy cannot be created nor destroyed. Initially, this was all in the gravitational potential energy store, but this is then transferred to the kinetic energy store once the pendulum starts to swing. At the bottom of the swing, the gravitational potential store will be greatly reduced and the energy will be mostly in the kinetic store. Some energy is also transferred to the surroundings as thermal energy by thermal transfer from friction due to air resistance, which must also be taken into consideration as part of the total energy of the system.

Eventually, the pendulum will stop swinging, so the gravitational energy has been transferred to kinetic energy and it has eventually all ended up in the surroundings by friction due to air resistance, leading to the surroundings becoming slightly warmer. The useful energy store has been dissipated to the surroundings.

Command word: Describe

When you are asked to **describe** something, you need to write down facts, events or processes accurately.

It is a good idea to state what the principle of conservation of energy is, so that the examiner knows that you understand it. You can then apply this idea to the changes in the energy stores and transfers in the system. It is also worth noting that the way we talk about energy at GCSE now has changed – you need to refer to energy stores as well as energy transfers. In this example, the main stores are gravitational and kinetic, and the motion of the pendulum is via mechanical transfer, with energy transfer to the surroundings by thermal transfer.

In energy transfers, the energy stores are usually dissipated to the surroundings, which become warmer. In a perfect situation, with no frictional forces or energy wasted, the pendulum would swing forever, but in reality this does not happen.

Refer to *energy stores* and *energy transfers* in your answer. There are eight energy stores and three energy transfers that you need to know. See page 1 to remind yourself of these.

Now try this

The people on a small island want to use either wind power, on hills and out at sea, or its reserves of coal to generate electrical energy. Describe the advantages and disadvantages of each resource. **(6 marks)**

Circuit symbols

Electric circuit diagrams are drawn using agreed symbols and conventions that can be understood by everybody across the world.

Circuit symbols

You need to know the symbols for these components.

Component	Symbol	Purpose
cell	positive terminal / negative terminal	provides a potential difference
battery		provides a potential difference
switches	open closed	allows the current flow to be switched on or off
voltmeter	—(V)—	measures potential difference across a component
ammeter	—(A)—	measures the current flowing through a component
fixed resistor		provides a fixed resistance to the flow of current
variable resistor		provides a variable (changeable) resistance
lamp	—(X)—	lights up when a current flows through it
fuse		wire melts if the current in a circuit gets too high
diode		allows current to flow in one direction only
thermistor		resistance decreases when the temperature increases
LDR		resistance decreases when the light intensity increases
LED		a diode that gives out light when current flows through it

Worked example

Name four components that are commonly used to change or control the amount of resistance in a circuit. **(2 marks)**

thermistor, LDR, fixed resistor, variable resistor

> 2 marks for all correct, 1 mark for 3 correct and zero marks for fewer than 3 correct.

Worked example

Describe how an LED is different from a filament lamp.   **(1 mark)**

An LED will only allow electrical current to pass through it in one direction.

> Think about what component is needed to detect the light, what the output device will be and how these will be connected to the cell.

Now try this

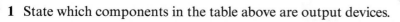

1 State which components in the table above are output devices.   **(2 marks)**

2 Design a circuit to turn on a lamp when it goes dark.   **(3 marks)**

3 State how ammeters and voltmeters should be arranged with components in circuits.   **(2 marks)**

Electrical charge and current

An **electric current** is the **rate of flow of charge**. In a metal, electric current is the flow of electrons.

Charge and current

The size of a current is a measure of how much charge flows past a point each second. It is the rate of flow of charge. The unit of charge is the **coulomb** (C). One ampere, or amp (A), is one coulomb of charge per second. You can calculate charge using the equation:

charge in C = current in A × time in s

$$Q = I t$$

LEARN IT!
IT'S NOT ON THE EQUATIONS LIST

Watch out! Don't get the units and quantities confused. The units have sensible abbreviations (C for coulombs, A for amps). The symbols for the quantities are not as easy to remember (Q stands for charge, I for current).

You also need to know how to rearrange the equation using the triangle shown so that you can calculate Q, I and t using values provided in questions.

Measuring current

Electric current will flow in a closed circuit when there is a source of potential difference. To measure the size of the current flowing through a component, an ammeter is connected in series with the component.

The current flowing is the same at all points in a series circuit. In this example, the current is 0.5 A.

The cell is the source of potential difference.

Conventional current flows this way, from + to − in a circuit.

Electrons flow this way, from − to +.

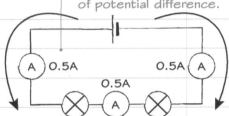

The three ammeters are connected in series with the two filament lamps.

Worked example

(a) Describe how ammeters should be connected with components in circuits. **(1 mark)**

Ammeters should always be arranged in series with the component to be measured.

(b) Describe what happens to the size of the current in a series circuit. **(1 mark)**

The current is the same value at any point in a series circuit.

Worked example

(a) A current of 1.5 A flows for 2 minutes. Calculate how much charge flows in this time. **(3 marks)**

$Q = I t$

$= 1.5\,A \times 120\,s = 180\,C$

(b) A charge of 1200 C flows through a filament lamp for 4 minutes. Calculate the average current in the filament lamp. **(3 marks)**

$I = Q \div t$

$= 1200\,C \div 240\,s$

$= 5\,A$

You can give the units of current as A or amps.

Now try this

1 Name the units of current and charge. **(2 marks)**

2 Calculate the charge that flows in one hour when there is a current of 0.25 A in a circuit. **(3 marks)**

3 A charge of 30 000 C is transferred by a current of 0.25 A. Calculate the length of time the current flows. **(4 marks)**

Current, resistance and potential difference

Ohm's law states how the **current** through a component relates to its **resistance** and the **potential difference** across it.

Resistance

The **resistance** of a component is a way of measuring how hard it is for electricity to flow through it. The units for resistance are **ohms (Ω)**.

The resistance of a whole circuit depends on the resistances of the different components in the circuit. The higher the total resistance, the smaller the current.

> resistance UP, current DOWN

The resistance of a circuit can be changed by putting different **resistors** into the circuit, or by using a **variable resistor**. The resistance of a variable resistor can be changed using a slider or knob.

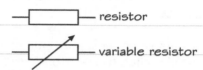

Ohm's law

Ohm's law states that the size of the current, I, flowing through a component of resistance, R, is directly proportional to the potential difference, V, across the component at constant temperature.

The equation for Ohm's law is:

potential difference in V = current in A × resistance in Ω

$$V = I R$$

LEARN IT!
IT'S NOT ON THE EQUATIONS LIST

Components that obey Ohm's law are said to be ohmic conductors whereas those that do not obey Ohm's law are non-ohmic. Examples of both of these can be found on page 15.

Worked example

(a) Resistor A has a resistance of 5 Ω and current of 3 A flowing through it. Calculate the size of the potential difference across resistor A. **(3 marks)**

$V = I R = 3A \times 5\Omega = 15V$

(b) Sketch a circuit that could be used to plot current against potential difference for this resistor. **(4 marks)**

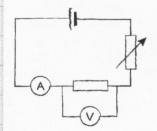

> The variable resistor can be used to collect numerous values for I and V so that an I–V graph can be plotted.

(c) Resistor A is then replaced with resistor B. A graph of current against potential difference is plotted. Explain what the graph tells you about the two resistors. **(2 marks)**

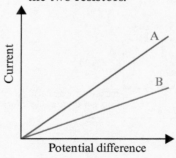

> The steeper line shows that resistor A has a lower resistance than resistor B.
>
> Both resistors are ohmic because the graphs are straight lines.

Now try this

> Rearrange the equation $V = I R$ to get R on its own.

1 A current of 3.2 A flows through a lamp of resistance 18 Ω. Calculate the size of the potential difference across the lamp. **(3 marks)**

2 The potential difference across a resistor is 28 V when the current flowing through it is 0.4 A. Calculate the resistance of the resistor. **(3 marks)**

Investigating resistance

🧪 **Practical skills** You can use appropriate circuits to investigate how combinations of resistors in series and parallel affect the overall electrical resistance in the circuit and how the length of a wire affects its resistance.

Required practical

There is more information relating to current, potential difference, resistance, and series and parallel circuits on pages 13 and 15–18.

Aim

to investigate electrical resistance in series and parallel circuits and how the resistance of a wire varies with its length

When resistors are arranged in series, potential difference is split across the resistors.

When resistors are arranged in parallel, the potential difference (pd) across each resistor will be the same as the power supply or battery pd.

Apparatus

battery or suitable power supply, ammeter, voltmeter, switch, crocodile clips, two resistors, resistance wire, metre ruler, variable resistor, connecting leads

Method 1: series and parallel

Set up the circuits in both series and parallel arrangements. Record the potential difference and current.

For both circuits, calculate the total effective resistance using the equation $R = V \div I$

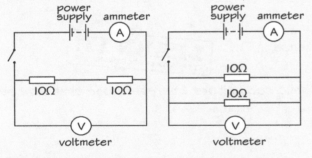

Work out the electrical resistance of each length of wire by dividing the potential difference value by the current value. Take repeat results (at least two sets) and then plot a graph of resistance on the y-axis against length on the x-axis.

Method 2: resistance of a wire

Set up the circuit shown in the diagram. Record the potential difference across the wire and the current in the wire for different lengths of wire.

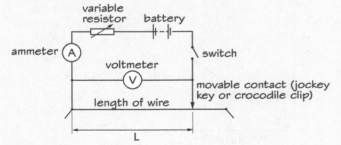

Now try this

1 Explain why it is good practice to obtain at least two sets of data when performing this investigation. **(4 marks)**
2 Explain why the total effective resistance is greater when resistors are arranged in series compared with being arranged in parallel. **(4 marks)**
3 Explain why it is a good idea to include a variable resistor and a switch in a circuit when investigating the relationship between resistance and length of a wire. **(4 marks)**

Results

Record your results for each method in a table similar to the one shown.

Length of wire in cm OR Arrangement of resistors	Potential difference in V	Current in A

Conclusion

The effective resistance when two resistors are connected in series is four times greater than when they are connected in parallel.

The resistance of the wire is directly proportional to its length. A graph of resistance against length should be a straight line through the origin.

Resistors

An **I–V graph** shows how the **current** flowing through a component varies as the **potential difference** across it varies. You need to know the characteristics of these I–V graphs.

① Fixed resistor

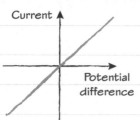

The temperature remains constant so the resistance remains constant. The slope or gradient is constant and the line remains straight throughout. Fixed resistors are ohmic conductors and show a linear relationship between current and potential difference.

② Filament lamp

Current ↑   Potential difference →

As the potential difference increases, the filament gets hotter, and atomic vibration increases. This leads to greater resistance. The slope or gradient decreases as the potential difference increases since resistance is increasing. The relationship is non-linear.

③ Diode

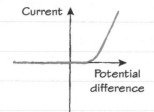

The current only flows in one direction. There is a **threshold** in the forward direction, which is why the graph is flat initially. A diode behaves like a fixed resistor – the resistance does not change. A diode has a very high resistance in the reverse direction.

Drawing an *I–V* graph

You can use a circuit like this to collect data about current and potential difference.

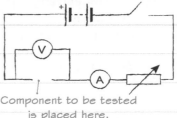

Component to be tested is placed here.

✓ When the switch is closed you can read current from the ammeter and potential difference from the voltmeter.

✓ Varying the value of the variable resistor allows you to record the current for different potential differences.

✓ You can reverse the cell to obtain negative values for potential difference.

Worked example

A student is testing the resistance of a component. She draws an *I–V* graph.

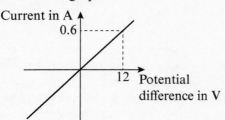

The component being tested is a
☐ diode
☐ filament lamp
☒ fixed resistor
☐ cell
(1 mark)

An *I–V* graph always has the current (*I*) plotted on the vertical *y*-axis and the potential difference (*V*) plotted on the horizontal *x*-axis. To find the resistance of a component from an *I–V* graph, you will need to divide the *x*-axis value by the corresponding *y*-axis value. That is, the gradient is not the resistance, the

$$\text{gradient} = \frac{1}{\text{resistance}}$$

Now try this

Amy is testing the resistance of a filament lamp. She varies the potential difference across the lamp and records the current that flows.

(a) Sketch a graph of potential difference (*V*) against current (*I*) for Amy's experiment.
(2 marks)

(b) Explain the shape of your graph. **(3 marks)**

15

LDRs and thermistors

The resistance of **light-dependent resistors (LDRs)** and **thermistors** changes according to light conditions (LDR) or temperature (thermistor).

Light-dependent resistors

The resistance of a **light-dependent resistor (LDR)** is large in the dark. The resistance gets less if light shines on it. The brighter the light, the lower the resistance. LDRs can be used to switch lights on when it gets dark.

brightness UP, resistance DOWN

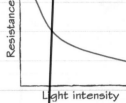

Thermistors

The resistance of a **thermistor** depends on its temperature. The higher the temperature, the lower the resistance. Thermistors can be used as a thermostat.

temperature UP, resistance DOWN

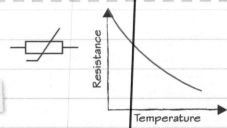

Worked example

A 6 V battery is connected in series with an LDR, a 300 Ω fixed resistor and an ammeter, as shown.

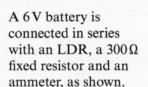

(a) Describe how the circuit shown can be used to explore the variation in resistance as the light levels change. **(2 marks)**

The amount of light being shone on the LDR can be changed by varying the intensity of the light it is exposed to from a torch or a lamp. The size of the current flowing in the circuit can then be recorded for each of these light levels.

(b) Describe the results you would expect. **(2 marks)**

The output current will be highest when the light level is greatest. As the brightness increases, the LDR's resistance decreases.

(c) How could a voltmeter be used in the circuit to show how the resistance changes with light levels? **(3 marks)**

Connect a voltmeter across the LDR. As the light level increases, the potential difference across the LDR will decrease since the resistance has decreased and a greater share of the 6 V will be across the fixed resistor.

Worked example

A 3 V battery is connected in series with a thermistor and an LDR, as shown.

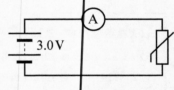

(a) Explain how the circuit can be used to explore how the resistance of the thermistor changes. **(2 marks)**

The thermistor could be immersed in a beaker of cold water, or a water bath, which is then heated from 10 °C to 80 °C. The current flowing in the circuit is recorded at each temperature over this range.

(b) Describe what your results would show. **(2 marks)**

As the temperature increases, the current increases. This is because the thermistor's resistance decreases as it gets warmer.

If a buzzer were placed in this circuit then it could be used as a simple fire alarm, with the buzzer sounding when the current reached a certain value. This could be controlled or calibrated by using a variable resistor.

Now try this

 1 State what affects the resistance of (a) a thermistor and (b) an LDR. **(2 marks)**

 2 Describe how an LDR and a thermistor could be used together in a circuit. **(4 marks)**

Investigating I–V characteristics

Practical skills   You can construct appropriate circuits to investigate the I–V characteristics of a variety of circuit elements, including a filament lamp, a diode and a resistor at constant temperature.

Required practical

> There is more information relating to current, potential difference and resistance in filament lamps, diodes and resistors on pages 13–16.

Aim

to investigate I–V graphs for a resistor, filament lamp and diode

Apparatus

ammeter, voltmeter, component holders, filament lamp, resistor, diode and protective resistor, variable resistor, switch, leads

> Be careful when using electrical circuits as electric current can produce heat and cause burns.

Method

Set up the circuits as shown and record the current through each component for different values of the potential difference (pd). The pd across each component is varied using the variable resistor. Reverse the cell or battery to obtain negative values for current and pd.

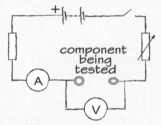

> In order to improve the accuracy of your results, place a switch in your circuit so that the current does not get too large. Too large a current leads to a greater value of the resistance being recorded, due to thermal energy causing extra vibrations of the ions in the metal lattice.

> Data collected in an investigation are accurate if close to the true value. The data are precise if the repeat readings of a certain variable are close to one another. The best data are both accurate and precise.

Results

Record your results in a table for each component. The results shown here are for the filament lamp.

Potential difference (V)	Current (I)
−2.0	−0.20
−1.5	−0.18
−1.0	−0.15
−0.5	−0.10
0	0
0.5	0.10
1.0	0.16
1.5	0.18
2.0	0.20

Draw a graph of current against potential difference.

> An I–V graph has current plotted on the y-axis and potential difference on the x-axis. The shape of the graph depends on the size or direction of the current through each component.

Conclusion

The I–V graphs for the components should look as shown on page 15.

Now try this

1 Explain why the I–V graph for a filament lamp has the shape that it does. **(5 marks)**

2 Explain why the I–V graph for the diode has the shape that it does. **(3 marks)**

3 Explain how the resistance of a resistor can be determined from an I–V graph. **(3 marks)**

Series and parallel circuits

Components can be arranged in series or parallel. The rules for current, potential difference and resistance are different for these two types of circuit.

Series circuits

A **series circuit** contains just one loop, around which an electric current can flow.

Adding more resistors in series means that the cell's potential difference is shared between more resistors. The current through the resistors decreases ($V = I\,R$), so the total resistance has increased.

The total resistance of two resistors arranged in series is equal to the sum of the resistance of each component, $R_{total} = R_1 + R_2$.

Ammeters are always connected in series with components.

Ammeters have a very low resistance so the current can flow through them and be measured accurately.

The size of the current in a series circuit is the same at every point in the circuit. All three ammeters in this circuit will show the same value for the current.

The potential difference across components that are arranged in series must add up to give the cell voltage, so $V_1 = V_2 + V_3$.

Voltmeters have a very high resistance so that no current will flow through them.

Parallel circuits

A **parallel circuit** contains more than one loop and the current will split up or recombine at the junctions.

The total resistance of two resistors arranged in parallel is less than the resistance of the smallest individual resistor.

Adding more resistors in parallel means that the cell's potential difference will be the same across each resistor. The total current increases, so the total resistance must have decreased.

The potential difference across the components in each branch of a parallel circuit must add up to give the cell voltage. The voltmeter readings across the two resistors will both have the same value as the potential difference across the cell.

The sum of the currents in each of the branches must equal the current leaving the cell. For this example, $A_1 = A_4 = A_2 + A_3$.

Worked example

What are the missing values in this parallel circuit if the bulbs are identical? **(2 marks)**

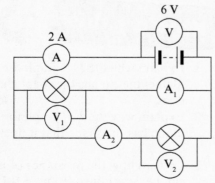

Both the ammeter readings A_1 and $A_2 = 1$ A. The voltmeter readings V_1 and V_2 will both be 6 V.

Now try this

1 Explain why car lights are connected in parallel and not in series. **(3 marks)**

2 Explain why a cell goes flat more quickly when lamps are arranged in parallel. **(4 marks)**

3 Two 20 Ω resistors are connected in series and then connected to a 12 V supply. Calculate:
 (a) the total resistance of the series arrangement **(2 marks)**
 (b) the current flowing in the circuit. **(3 marks)**

ac and dc

Circuits can be operated using **alternating current (ac)** or **direct current (dc)**.

Direct current

An **electric current** in a wire is a flow of electrons. The current supplied by **cells** and **batteries** is **direct current (dc)**. In a direct current the electrons all flow in the same direction.

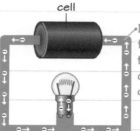

cell

Electrons are pushed out of one end of the cell.

Electrons flow round to the other end of the cell.

There must be a complete circuit for the electrons to flow.

The oscilloscope trace for dc from a battery is a horizontal line. The potential difference can be read off the vertical scale.

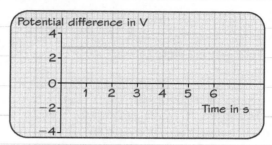

The potential difference above has a constant value of 2.8 V.

Alternating current

Mains electricity supplied to homes and businesses is an **alternating current (ac)**. Alternating current is an electric current that changes direction regularly, and its potential difference is constantly changing.

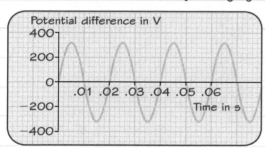

For an ac supply, the movement of charge is constantly changing direction. The mains supply has an average working value of 230 V and a frequency of 50 Hz. This means that the electric current and voltage change direction 100 times every second.

dc and ac supply in the home

Both dc and ac can be used in the home; dc is supplied in the form of cells and batteries, ac is the mains supply. Both can be used by devices to transfer energy to motors and heating devices.

Different electrical appliances have different power ratings. The power rating tells you how much energy is transferred by the appliance each second.

Appliance	Power rating
kettle	2200 W
hairdryer	1500 W
microwave	850 W
electric oven	3000 W
electric shaver	15 W

Now try this

1 Give **three** examples of devices that use
   (a) dc   **(3 marks)**
   (b) ac.   **(3 marks)**

2 Describe how ac and dc are
   (a) similar   **(1 mark)**
   (b) different.   **(2 marks)**

Mains electricity

Electrical energy enters UK homes as mains electricity at 230V ac. Most electrical appliances are connected to the mains using a three-core cable.

Live, neutral and earth wires

The live, neutral and earth wires are made from copper, but covered in colour-coded insulating plastic so that the consumer is not exposed to a dangerous voltage.

The neutral (blue) wire completes the circuit with the appliance. It is at a potential difference of 0V with respect to the earth wire.

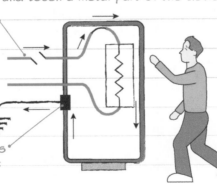

The live (brown) wire carries the supply to the appliance. It is at a potential difference of 230V with respect to the neutral and earth wires.

The earth (yellow and green) wire does not form part of the circuit but acts as a safety feature along with the fuse.

Earthing

A live wire may be dangerous even when a switch in the mains circuit is open. If a person touches a metal device that is live, current would flow through him to earth and could be fatal. Appliances are earthed so that a user cannot be electrocuted.

1 The live wire inside the appliance may come loose and touch a metal part of the device's casing.

2 The large current heats and melts the wire in the fuse, making a break in the circuit.

5 By having an earth wire connected to the metal casing, the user is not at risk if the live wire comes loose and touches anything metallic.

3 The earth wire is connected to the metal casing and a large current flows in through the live wire and out through the earth wire.

4 The circuit is no longer complete, so there is no chance of electric shock or fire.

Worked example

Describe how two safety devices keep the user safe when using mains electricity. **(4 marks)**

A fuse will melt if the current through it gets too high, so the appliance cannot overheat and will be isolated at 0V.

If the live wire touches the metal case, a large current will pass through the fuse to the earth wire. The fuse melts, reducing the potential difference to 0V and making it impossible to be electrocuted.

Potential differences

The potential difference between the wires in the mains supply has different values.

Wires	Potential difference in V
live and earth	230
live and neutral	230
earth and neutral	0

Now try this

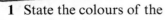

1 State the colours of the
  (a) live wire   **(1 mark)**
  (b) neutral wire   **(1 mark)**
  (c) earth wire.   **(1 mark)**

2 Describe how an earth wire and fuse protect the user when the live wire comes loose.
   (4 marks)

3 Explain why the earth wire is not normally part of the circuit in a mains appliance. **(3 marks)**

Electrical power

Electrical power is the amount of electrical energy that is transferred to other energy stores each second.

Calculating power

Power is the energy transferred per second or the rate at which energy is transferred. It is measured in **watts**. For electrical devices, power depends on the current in the device and the potential difference across it, or the resistance of the device. It also depends on the total energy transferred and the time taken to transfer the energy.

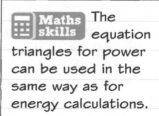 The **Maths skills** equation triangles for power can be used in the same way as for energy calculations.

There are three equations you need to know that can be used to calculate power:

1   power in W = current in A × potential difference in V
$$P = I\,V$$

 **LEARN IT!** IT'S NOT ON THE EQUATIONS LIST

2   power in W = current squared in A² × resistance in Ω
$$P = I^2\,R$$

 **LEARN IT!** IT'S NOT ON THE EQUATIONS LIST

3   power in W = energy transferred in J ÷ time taken in s
$$P = E \div t$$

 **LEARN IT!** IT'S NOT ON THE EQUATIONS LIST

Worked example

Calculate the power rating of a microwave that transfers 30 000 J of electrical energy in 35 s. **(3 marks)**

$P = E \div t$

$= 30\,000\,J \div 35\,s = 857\,W$ (or 857 J/s)

Worked example

An electric oven is connected to the mains at a potential difference of 230 V and takes a current of 30 A. Calculate the power rating of the oven. **(3 marks)**

$P = I\,V$

$= 30\,A × 230\,V = 6900\,W$ (or 6900 J/s)

Worked example

A current of 4 A passes through a wire of resistance 55 Ω. Work out how much energy is transferred each second. **(3 marks)**

Energy transferred per second is power.

$P = I^2\,R$

$= (4\,A)^2 × 55\,Ω$

$P = 880\,W$ or (880 J/s)

 Remember that an energy transfer of 1 joule per second (J/s) is equal to a power of 1 watt (W).

Worked example

A device has a power rating of 3400 W and a resistance of 120 Ω. Calculate the size of the current flowing in the device. **(4 marks)**

$P = I^2\,R$

Rearranging gives $I = \sqrt{\dfrac{P}{R}}$

$= \sqrt{\dfrac{3400\,W}{120\,Ω}} = 5.3\,A$

You may need to rearrange equations to make I, R or V the subject of the formula.

Now try this

1   Calculate the power of a device that transfers 400 000 J of energy in 200 seconds. **(3 marks)**
2   Calculate the current that flows in a 3000 W oven when connected to the 230 V mains supply. **(3 marks)**
3   An appliance has a resistance of 470 Ω and a power rating of 2000 W. Calculate the size of the current that flows in the appliance. **(4 marks)**

Electrical energy

Everyday electrical appliances are designed to bring about energy transfers. You need to know the equations that link energy to power, time, charge and potential difference.

Power of a device

The power of a device is related to:
- the potential difference across it and the current through it
- the energy transferred over a given time.

A device that transfers more energy in a shorter time has a higher power.

Energy, charge and potential difference

Energy, charge and potential difference are related by the equation:

$$\begin{array}{ccc} \text{energy} & \text{charge} & \text{potential} \\ \text{transferred} = & \text{flow} \times & \text{difference} \\ \text{in J} & \text{in C} & \text{in V} \end{array}$$

$$E = Q\,V$$

LEARN IT!
IT'S NOT ON THE EQUATIONS LIST

Calculate the charge, Q, from the current reading on the ammeter using the equation $Q = I\,t$ (see page 12).

Remember that for this circuit, the value obtained for the energy transferred will be for this bulb, since the potential difference being measured is across this bulb only.

The potential difference, V, across the bulb is measured with a voltmeter. Voltmeters are always connected in parallel with components and ammeters are always connected in series.

Power and stored energy

An appliance with a higher power rating transfers more energy to other energy stores each second than an appliance with a lower power rating.

For example, a kettle has a power rating of 2 kW and so will transfer much more energy to the thermal store of the surroundings than a light bulb with a power rating of 10 W, in the same time.

Maths skills Cover up the quantity you want to find with your finger. The position of the other two quantities tells you the formula.

Work is done when charge flows in a circuit.

Worked example

(a) A charge of 25 C passes through a motor. The potential difference across the motor is 6 V. Calculate how much energy is transferred. **(3 marks)**

$E = Q\,V$, so $E = 25\,C \times 6\,V = 150\,J$

(b) A current of 1.2 A flows through a bulb for 2 minutes. The potential difference across the bulb is 12 V. Work out how much energy is transferred. **(3 marks)**

$E = Q\,V$ and $Q = I\,t$, so $E = I\,t\,V$

$E = 1.2\,A \times 120\,s \times 12\,V = 1728\,J$

(c) A charge of 18 C transfers 364 J of electrical energy through a resistor. Calculate the potential difference across the resistor. **(3 marks)**

Rearrange $E = Q\,V$ to give $V = E \div Q$

$V = 364\,J \div 18\,C = 20.2\,V$

Now try this

1 A charge of 24 C flows through an LED and the potential difference across it is 6 V. Calculate how much energy is transferred. **(3 marks)**

2 Explain why the volt, V, can also be described as a 'joule per coulomb'. **(3 marks)**

3 Calculate the amount of charge required to transfer 2800 J of energy when a potential difference of 14 V is applied across a filament lamp. **(3 marks)**

The National Grid

The **National Grid** is a system of wires that **transmits electricity** from power stations to where the electricity is needed and used.

The National Grid

Electricity is generated and transported to our homes, hospitals and factories by the National Grid. The National Grid is the **wires** and **transformers** that transmit the electricity; it does **not** include the **power stations** and the **consumers**.

To ensure that transmission is efficient, and that very little energy is lost as heat, the voltage and current values need to be chosen carefully at different stages.

Efficient energy transfer

Electricity is transmitted at a high voltage and a low current because less energy is wasted as thermal energy when the current is kept low. The equation $P = I^2R$ shows that, if the current is halved, then the power wasted as thermal energy is a quarter of what was wasted before $(\frac{1}{2} \times \frac{1}{2} = \frac{1}{4})$.

The power wasted as thermal energy transferred to the surroundings is proportional to I^2. If the current gets 10 times bigger, then 100 times more energy will be lost as heat each second.

Transformers and the National Grid

1 **Fossil fuels** or **nuclear fuel** are often used to generate electrical energy in the power station.

2 A **step-up transformer** increases the voltage to 132 kV or more. For a fixed amount of electrical energy or power output, increasing the voltage means there will be a decrease in current. Electrical energy is transmitted at a high voltage and low current through the wires to reduce energy losses as heat in the wires. It also means thinner wires can be used, which reduces costs.

3 **Step-down transformers** decrease the voltages from the National Grid for safer use in our homes and industry. Reducing the voltage means that there will be an increase in current.

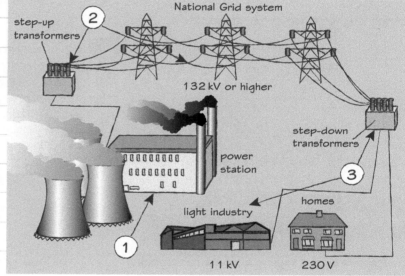

Worked example

Explain why electrical power is transmitted at a high voltage and a low current on the National Grid. **(3 marks)**

Power is transmitted at a high voltage and a low current because the amount of electrical energy wasted as thermal energy is proportional to the square of the current, from the equation $P = I^2R$. So, if we double the size of the current flowing, the power wasted increases by a factor of 2^2 or 4.

Now try this

1 (a) Describe what the National Grid is. **(2 marks)**
  (b) Explain what it is used for. **(2 marks)**
2 Describe the role played by transformers in the National Grid. **(4 marks)**

Static electricity

Static electricity occurs when electric charges are transferred **onto**, or **off**, the surface of an **insulator**. This causes the insulator to gain a positive or a **negative** charge.

Negatively charged insulators

Insulators become **negatively charged** when **electrons** move **onto** the **insulator** from the cloth due to **friction**.

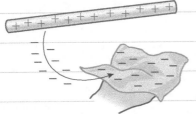

polythene rod

Negative rod, **positive** cloth

When **polythene** is rubbed with a cloth, electrons are transferred by **friction** from the **cloth** to the **rod**. Since electrons are **negatively** charged, the rod becomes **negatively charged** and the cloth becomes positively **charged**. These charges are **equal** and **opposite**.

It is **always** the **electron** that is transferred when insulators become charged by friction.

Positively charged insulators

Insulators become positively charged when electrons move **off** the **insulator** and onto the cloth due to the force of **friction**.

When **acetate** is rubbed with a cloth, electrons are transferred by **friction** from the **rod** to the **cloth**. Again, since electrons are **negatively** charged, the **cloth** becomes **negatively charged** and the **acetate rod** becomes positively **charged**. Again, these charges will be **equal** and **opposite**.

Positive rod, **negative** cloth

Worked example

Describe what happens when two electrically charged objects are brought close together.

(3 marks)

 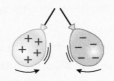

The charged objects exert a force on each other. If the two objects have the same type of electrical charge they repel each other. If they have different types of electrical charge they attract each other.

Now try this

1 What charge will an insulator have if it
   (a) gains electrons **(1 mark)**
   (b) loses electrons? **(1 mark)**

2 Which objects will attract each other?
   ☐ two negatively charged rods
   ☐ a positively charged duster and a negatively charged rod
   ☐ two positively charged objects
   ☐ a neutral rod and a neutral duster. **(1 mark)**

3 Explain why insulators never become charged by gaining or losing protons. **(3 marks)**

4 Polythene gains electrons when rubbed. Describe how you could use a polythene rod to tell if an insulator were positively charged. **(3 marks)**

Electric fields

An **electric field** is a region in space where a **charged particle** may experience a **force**.

Electric field from a point charge

The **electric field** from a **positive point charge** acts **radially outwards**.

The **electric field** from a **negative point charge** acts **radially inwards**.

Electric field strength is a **vector** quantity because it has both a **size** and a **direction**. The arrows show the direction that a **positive charge** would move in if it were placed in the field.

A positive charge in the field around a negative charge would move towards the negative charge, since positive and negative charges attract.

An electric field is created in the region around a charged particle. The charged particle will experience a non-contact force. A negatively charged electron placed in the electric field around a positively charged nucleus will experience a non-contact force that attracts it towards the positive charge. This explains why materials can gain electrons when they are rubbed, and explains why we encounter static electricity in nature.

Only electrons are transferred when an insulator becomes charged. If a material gains electrons it becomes negatively charged; if it loses electrons it becomes positively charged.

Showing the strength of the field

The strength of an electric field is shown by the concentration of the field lines. The more concentrated the lines, the stronger the electric field.

| weak positive point charge | weak negative point charge | strong negative point charge |

An electrostatic force is a non-contact force – the objects do not need to be in contact to feel the effect of the force.

Sparking

Electrons can be transferred onto your clothes by friction. The electrons will stay on your clothes because clothes are insulators – the electrons cannot flow off. However, if you then touch a metal door handle, the electrons can conduct to earth as a spark. The electrons will move off your clothes because there is a potential difference between your negatively charged clothes and the earth at 0 V.

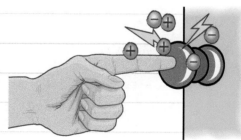

Worked example

Explain what will happen to a proton that is placed in the electric field of a positive point charge. **(3 marks)**

A proton is a positively charged particle, so it will be repelled by the positive charge and move outwards. Since the proton will experience a resultant force, it will accelerate.

Now try this

1 Describe how the motion of a charged particle changes in an electric field when:
   (a) its mass changes **(2 marks)**
   (b) it is given the opposite charge. **(2 marks)**
2 Explain how electric fields provide an explanation of static electricity. **(4 marks)**

Extended response – Electricity

There will be at least one 6-mark question on your exam paper. For these questions, you will need to think scientifically and structure your answer logically, showing how the points you make are related to each other. You can revise the topics for this question, which is about **electricity**, on pages 11–25.

Worked example

Two identical bulbs can be connected to a 6 V cell in series or parallel as shown in the diagram.
Compare the brightness of the bulbs in the two circuits when the switches are closed.
Your answer should refer to the current, potential difference, energy stores and rates of energy transfer in both circuits.

 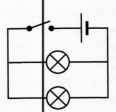

(6 marks)

The brightness of the bulbs in the series circuit will be much less than the brightness of the bulbs in the parallel circuit.

The electrical energy that is transferred to light is directly proportional to the potential difference across each bulb and the size of the current flowing through each bulb. The brightness of the bulbs will be greatest when the energy transferred per second is greatest.

In the series circuit, the potential difference across each bulb will be 3 V, whereas in the parallel circuit the potential difference across each bulb will be 6 V. Also, the current flowing through each of the bulbs in the parallel circuit will be greater than the current flowing through the bulbs in the series circuit. Since the current and the potential difference in the parallel bulbs are greater, more energy will be transferred per second and the bulb will be brighter.

 The opening sentence simply states how the brightness of the lamps compares in each of the two circuits.

 The answer then states the relationship between electrical energy, current and potential difference before relating brightness to the energy transferred per second, or power, of the bulbs.

 The comparison of the bulbs' brightness is related to the relative sizes of any current, potential difference and energy transferred per second.

The rate at which energy is transferred from one form to another is called power. When dealing with electrical circuits, the power is calculated using the equation $P = IV$. You can read more about this on page 21.

Now try this

You have been provided with a circuit component, but you are unsure what the component is. Describe how you could conduct an experiment to try to determine what the component is. Refer to any apparatus you would use, any results you would collect and any graphs you would draw.   **(6 marks)**

Density

The **density** of a material is a measure of the **amount of matter** that it contains **per unit volume**.

Density, mass and volume

Changing the amount of material will change both its mass and its volume. If the volume of a block of a particular material is doubled, its mass will also double.

The density of a material does not vary greatly for a given state of matter and relates to how closely packed the atoms or molecules are within the volume that it occupies.

The density of a material in the different states of matter varies greatly because of the arrangement of the particles in the state.

solid   liquid   gas

In a solid, the particles are closely packed together. The number of particles in a given volume is high. Solids are high density.

In a liquid, the particles are usually less densely packed than in a solid. The number of particles in a given volume is less than for a solid.

In a gas, the particles are spread out. The number of particles in a given volume is low. Gases are low density.

Calculating density

You can calculate density using the equation:

$$\text{density in kg/m}^3 = \frac{\text{mass in kg}}{\text{volume in m}^3}$$

$$\rho = \frac{m}{V}$$

LEARN IT!
IT'S NOT ON THE EQUATIONS LIST

Changing the volume of a substance will change its mass, but its density will be constant.

Other units for density can also be used, such as g/cm^3. The density of copper is $8.96\,g/cm^3$. This means that every $1\,cm^3$ of copper metal has a mass of $8.96\,g$.

Worked example

(a) A body has a mass of 34 000 kg and a volume of 18 m³. Calculate its density. **(4 marks)**

density = mass ÷ volume
= 34 000 kg ÷ 18 m³
= 1900 kg/m³

(b) Calculate the mass of 0.2 m³ of this material. **(4 marks)**

mass = density × volume
= 1900 kg/m³ × 0.2 m³ = 380 kg

🖩 Maths skills — Using correct units

When performing calculations involving density, mass and volume check that:
- you are using the correct equation to find density, mass or volume.
- the units are consistent.

When the mass is in kg and the volume is in m³ then the density will be in kg/m³. Sometimes you may be dealing with g and cm³, so check the units.

Worked example

A solid has a density of 3600 kg/m³ and a mass of 0.32 kg. Calculate its volume. **(4 marks)**

volume = mass ÷ density
= 0.32 kg ÷ 3600 kg/m³ = 0.00009 m³

🖩 Maths skills — Checking units

Since volume = mass ÷ density then the units here will be kg ÷ kg/m³. This is the same as kg × m³/kg, which means the kilograms cancel and we are left with m³ – a unit of volume.

Now try this

1 Calculate the density of a material that has a mass of 84 kg and a volume of 0.075 m³.
(3 marks)

2 The density of aluminium is 2700 kg/m³. Calculate the mass of a block of aluminium with a volume of 0.05 m³.
(3 marks)

Investigating density

Practical skills You can measure the volume and mass of solids and liquids to determine their densities.

Required practical

Aim

to determine the density of solids and liquids

Apparatus

measuring cylinder, displacement can, electronic balance, ruler, various solids and liquids

Method 1 (for a solid)

1 Measure the mass of the solid using an electronic balance and record its mass in your results table.

2 Determine the volume of the solid. This can be done by measuring its dimensions and using a formula, or by using a displacement can to see how much liquid it displaces. Record this value in your results table. You can also use method 2 if the object will fit into a measuring cylinder.

Method 2 (for a liquid)

1 Find the mass of the liquid by placing the measuring cylinder on the scales, and then zeroing the scales with no liquid present in the measuring cylinder. Add the liquid to the desired level.

2 Record the mass of the liquid in g from the balance and its volume in cm³ from the measuring cylinder.

Be careful to read the volume value correctly – at the bottom of the meniscus.

Results

Your results can be recorded in a table.

Material	Mass in g	Volume in cm³	Density in g/cm³

Find the density of the solid by using the equation

$$\text{density} = \frac{\text{mass}}{\text{volume}}$$

Conclusion

The density of a solid and a liquid can be determined by finding their respective masses and volumes. Dividing the mass by the volume gives you the density of the solid or liquid. The results should be compared with published values.

There is more information about the relationship between mass, volume and density on page 27.

Be careful to use solids and liquids that are safe to use in this investigation. Mercury (a liquid metal) was used in these investigations until it was found to be carcinogenic.

When taking volume readings, make sure that you read the scales with your eye at the same level as the meniscus. Otherwise a parallax error will arise and your values will be incorrect.

Maths skills Converting between units

Density can be given in g/cm³ or kg/m³.

Since 1 kg = 1000 g and 1 m³ = 1 000 000 cm³:
- to convert from g/cm³ to kg/m³ multiply by 1000
- to convert from kg/m³ to g/cm³ divide by 1000.

For example, water has a density of 1 g/cm³ or 1000 kg/m³.

Now try this

1 A measuring cylinder is placed on an electronic balance and its display is set to zero. The measuring cylinder is then filled with a liquid up to a volume of 256 cm³. The mass shown is 454 g. Calculate the density of the liquid.
(3 marks)

2 Explain how misreading the mass and volume values may occur and how this can lead to a higher-than-normal density value. **(4 marks)**

Changes of state

Substances can change from one state of matter to another. The **change of state** depends on whether **energy is gained** or **lost** by the substance.

The three states of matter

solid

In a solid the particles vibrate but they cannot move freely.

liquid

In a liquid the particles can move past each other and move around randomly.

gas

In a gas the particles move around very fast and they move all the time. This is because they have a lot of kinetic energy.

Changing state

Changes of state are physical changes rather than chemical changes and they can be reversed.

The mass before the change is equal to the mass after the change. For example, when 500 kg of a solid melts it becomes 500 kg of a liquid.

When a body is heated or cooled, its temperature will change if its state of matter does not change. For example, if 750 ml of a liquid is heated, then the temperature will increase until it reaches its boiling point.

When a material changes state, it does so at a constant temperature. For example, when water boils, 1 kg of water at 100°C will turn into 1 kg of steam at 100°C. For more about this, see page 3.

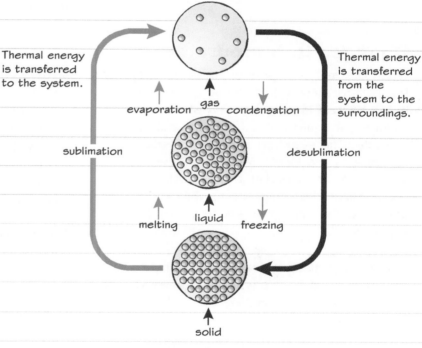

Thermal energy is transferred to the system.

Thermal energy is transferred from the system to the surroundings.

evaporation   gas   condensation

sublimation   desublimation

melting   liquid   freezing

solid

Worked example

Describe what happens when 2.0 kg of steam is allowed to cool against a glass plate, collected and then placed in a freezer. **(4 marks)**

2.0 kg of water will be produced when the steam turns to water at 100°C. It will then cool as a liquid from 100°C to room temperature. When placed in the freezer it will cool down from room temperature and turn to ice at 0°C before continuing to cool to around −18°C.

Now try this

1 Describe what happens when 1.5 kg of ice is left on a kitchen bench. **(3 marks)**

2 Explain why a change of state is a physical change and not a chemical change. **(2 marks)**

3 Describe what happens when 200 kg of solid copper is heated to beyond its boiling point. **(5 marks)**

Internal energy

Internal energy is the energy stored in a system by its particles.

Internal energy

The internal energy of a system has two parts:

1 The kinetic energy of the particles based on their motion, relative to each other.

2 The potential energy of the particles based on the relative positions of the particles.

$$\text{internal energy} = \text{kinetic energy of particles} + \text{potential energy of particles}$$

Changing internal energy

Internal energy can be changed by changing the kinetic energy of the particles or the potential energy of the particles in the system.

Heating the system increases the energy stored within it by increasing the energy of the particles within it.

If the kinetic energy of the particles increases, then the temperature of the system will increase. When the system changes state, there will be a change to the potential energy of the particles but the kinetic energy will not change.

Changes in temperature

When thermal energy is supplied to a system, the temperature will increase if the material being heated is not changing state – for example, if liquid water is being heated in a kettle. The supplied energy leads to an increase in the kinetic energy of the water molecules. The greater their kinetic energy, the greater the temperature will be. To calculate the change in energy, use the equation:

$$\text{energy in J} = \text{mass in kg} \times \text{specific heat capacity in J/kg°C} \times \text{temperature change in °C}$$

You can find out more about this on page 3.

Changes in state

When thermal energy is supplied to a system, it may result in a change of state – for example when ice is heated to become the same mass of liquid water.

When this change of state occurs, the temperature remains constant – for water this is 0°C. There will be no overall change in the kinetic energy of the water molecules when this happens but there will be an increase in the overall potential energy of the water molecules. To calculate the change in energy, use the equation:

$$\text{energy in J} = \text{mass in kg} \times \text{specific latent heat in J/kg}$$

You can find out more about this on page 31.

Worked example

Explain what happens to the internal energy when a gas is heated. **(3 marks)**

When a gas is heated, thermal energy is supplied to the molecules in the system. This causes the kinetic energy of the molecules to increase, which leads to a change in temperature. This increase in energy can be calculated using the equation $\Delta E = m\,c\,\Delta\theta$.

Worked example

Explain what happens to the internal energy of water vapour when it condenses to become liquid water at 100°C. **(3 marks)**

When the water vapour turns into liquid water at 100°C there will not be a change in the kinetic energy of the water molecules, so the temperature will not change, but there will be a decrease in the potential energy of the water molecules as they move from a gas state to a liquid state. This energy can be calculated using the equation $E = m\,L$.

Now try this

1 Explain what can happen to a system when the kinetic energy of its particles changes. **(3 marks)**

2 Explain what happens to the internal energy of liquid steel when it cools and becomes a solid. **(4 marks)**

Specific latent heat

Specific latent heat relates to the energy involved when a material changes state.

Specific latent heat

Specific latent heat is the **energy** that must be transferred to change **1 kg** of a material from **one state of matter to another**. There are usually two values for specific latent heat:

1 the **specific latent heat of fusion** when the change of state is between a solid and a liquid – during **melting** or **freezing**

2 the **specific latent heat of vaporisation** when the change of state is between a liquid and a gas – during **boiling** or **condensation**.

You can calculate the thermal energy required using the equation:

thermal energy for a change of state in J = mass in kg × specific latent heat in J/kg

$$E = m\,L$$

Specific latent heat should **not** be confused with specific heat capacity. Calculations involving **specific latent heat** involve changes of state and **never involve a change in temperature**, since **changes of state always occur** at a **constant temperature**.

Specific latent heat of fusion

For water, this value is 334 000 J/kg. This means that 334 000 J need to be supplied to melt 1 kg of ice or 334 000 J need to be lost to convert 1 kg of water to ice.

Specific latent heat of vaporisation

For water, this value is 2 260 000 J/kg. So 2 260 000 J of energy need to be supplied to convert 1 kg of water to 1 kg of steam at 100 °C and 2 260 000 J need to be lost to convert 1 kg of steam to liquid water at 100 °C.

Worked example

(a) Ice at –40 °C is heated until it becomes steam at 110 °C. Sketch a graph to show the changes that take place during this process.

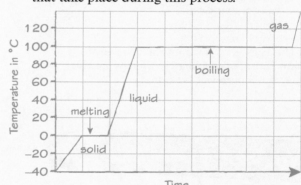

(b) Explain when the equations for specific latent heat would be used to calculate any energy changes. **(3 marks)**

The equations for specific latent heat would be used when the ice is melting at 0 °C and when the water is boiling at 100 °C. This is because the potential energy changes during a change of state and not the kinetic energy, so there would be no change in temperature.

Worked example

(a) Calculate the amount of energy required to convert 25 kg of ice to water at 0 °C. **(3 marks)**

$E = m\,L = 25\,kg × 334\,000\,J/kg$
$= 8\,350\,000\,J$

(b) Calculate the amount of energy required to convert 40 kg of steam to liquid water at 100 °C. **(3 marks)**

$E = m\,L = 40\,kg × 2\,260\,000\,J/kg$
$= 90\,400\,000\,J$

Use the correct value of *L* for the change of state involved in each case.

Now try this

 1 Calculate the energy required to convert 50 kg of ice into water at 0 °C. **(3 marks)**

2 Calculate the energy required to convert 25 kg of water into steam at 100 °C. **(3 marks)**

Particle motion in gases

The **pressure** of a **gas** can be explained in terms of the motion of its particles.

The pressure of a gas

Gas pressure depends on the motion of the particles in the gas. Gas particles strike the walls of a container at many different angles. So the pressure of a gas produces a net force at right angles to the wall.

Pressure can be increased by:
- **increasing** the **temperature** of the gas
- **increasing** the **mass** of the gas
- **decreasing** the **volume** of the gas.

Pressure and temperature

The **pressure** of a **fixed mass** of **gas** at a **constant volume** depends on the **temperature** of the gas. When the temperature increases:

1. The gas molecules have a greater average kinetic energy.
2. The gas molecules move faster.
3. There are more collisions between the molecules and the walls of the container each second.
4. More force is exerted on the same area each second.
5. The pressure of the gas increases.

Volume and temperature

For a fixed mass of gas inside a balloon, the number of gas molecules will be constant. The particles are in constant random motion.

If the gas is at a constant temperature then the average kinetic energy of the gas molecules will be constant.

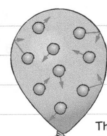

By increasing the temperature of the gas, the average kinetic energy of the gas molecules will increase.

The gas molecules will make more collisions with the inner surface of the balloon. The volume of the balloon then increases.

Worked example

Explain gas pressure using kinetic theory.   **(3 marks)**

The particles (atoms or molecules) in a gas are continuously moving in a random way and colliding with the container walls. The force from these collisions produces pressure on the walls. On average the number and force of collisions are the same in all directions, so pressure is the same on all the walls of the container.

Worked example

The motion of the particles in a gas is described as random. Explain what is meant by the term random.   **(2 marks)**

Random means that it is impossible to predict the motion of any of the individual particles in the gas – they can be travelling in different directions and at different speeds but this motion cannot be determined accurately.

Now try this

1 The temperature of a fixed amount of gas increases from 200 °C to 300 °C. Describe what happens to the average kinetic energy of the particles in this gas.   **(2 marks)**

2 (a) State what happens to the average speed of gas particles as a gas is cooled.   **(1 mark)**
   (b) Explain the effect this has on the pressure of the gas in a rigid sealed container.   **(2 marks)**

Pressure in gases

The **change in the volume** of a gas is **inversely proportional** to the change in pressure when the mass and temperature are constant.

Changing the volume of a gas at constant temperature

Pressure and **volume** are **inversely proportional** to each other.

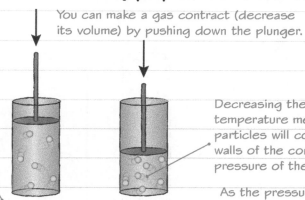

You can make a gas contract (decrease its volume) by pushing down the plunger.

A gas can be compressed or expanded by pressure changes. The pressure produces a net force at right angles to the wall of the gas container (or any surface).

The product of pressure and volume, $p \times V$, will always have the same value.

Decreasing the volume of a gas at a constant temperature means that the moving gas particles will collide more frequently with the walls of the container they are in. The pressure of the gas will increase.

10 m³ × 100 kPa = 1 000 000 Pa

5 m³ × 200 kPa = 1 000 000 Pa

As the pressure increases then the volume of the gas must decrease if the temperature of the gas is kept constant.

Gas equation

You can use this equation to calculate the pressure or volume of gases for a fixed mass of gas at a constant temperature:

pressure in Pa × volume in m³ = constant

pV = constant

You can use this equation to calculate the new pressure and volume of a fixed mass of gas at a constant temperature when the pressure or volume changes. The SI base units for p are pascals (Pa) and for V are m³.
1 kPa = 1000 Pa

The units for pressure and volume do not have to be in SI units as long as the same units are used throughout.

See page 60 for more on pressure.

See page 60 for more on pressure.

Worked example

At atmospheric pressure, 100 kPa, the volume of the column of trapped gas in the apparatus shown is 28 cm³. The pump is used to increase the pressure on the trapped gas to 250 kPa. Calculate the new volume of the trapped air. **(4 marks)**

Rearrange the equation given on the left to give:

pressure × volume before change = pressure × volume after change

so $p_1 V_1 = p_2 V_2$ and

where $V_1 = 28\,cm^3$, $p_1 = 100\,kPa$ and
$p_2 = 250\,kPa$

$$V_2 = \frac{28\,cm^3 \times 100\,kPa}{250\,kPa} = 11.2\,cm^3$$

Worked example

At atmospheric pressure, 100 kPa, the volume of trapped gas in a syringe is 48 cm³. The gas is then compressed to a new volume of 18 cm³. Calculate the new pressure of the gas. **(4 marks)**

Using the equation from the Worked example above:

$p_1 V_1 = p_2 V_2$

where $V_1 = 48\,cm^3$, $p_1 = 100\,kPa$ and $V_2 = 18\,cm^3$.

$$p_2 = \frac{100\,kPa\ 48\,cm^3}{18\,cm^3} = 267\,kPa$$

Now try this

1 If $p_1 = 200\,kPa$ and $V_1 = 28\,cm^3$, calculate the new pressure p_2 when the volume is increased to 44.8 cm³. **(3 marks)**

2 Explain how it is possible for a gas to be compressed at a constant temperature. **(2 marks)**

3 A gas, initially at a pressure of 200 kPa, occupies a volume of 480 m³. Calculate the new volume of the gas when the pressure decreases to 120 kPa at constant temperature. **(4 marks)**

Extended response – Particle model

There will be at least one 6-mark question on your exam paper. For these questions, you will need to think scientifically and structure your answer logically, showing how the points you make are related to each other. You can revise the topics for this question, which is about the **particle model**, on pages 27–33.

Worked example

A team of investigators has been asked to determine whether rings being sold in a jeweller's shop are made from pure gold or whether they are fake.

Explain how the investigators could determine whether the rings were made from pure gold, which has a density of 19.3 g/cm³.

Your answer should refer to a suitable experimental method that will allow you to determine the density of the material and any equations you would need to use. **(6 marks)**

Density = mass ÷ volume; it is the mass per unit volume of a material. It is fixed for a substance in a given phase of matter.

To find the mass of a ring, we would put it on the electronic balance and get its mass in grams. To find the volume of the ring, we would lower it into a measuring cylinder of water and find the difference in the volume readings on the measuring cylinder scale. We do this by subtracting the volume reading before the ring has been submerged in the water from the volume reading after the ring has been submerged. This difference in volume is equal to the volume of the ring in cm³. Dividing the value for the mass of the ring in g by the volume of the ring in cm³ will get the value for the density of the ring in g/cm³.

If the value obtained for the density is very close to 19.3 g/cm³ then the ring *might be* made from gold. If the density is very different from the value of 19.3 g/cm³ then it is not pure gold.

> The answer starts with a brief explanation of what density is, as well as stating the equation.

> The method addresses how the mass and volume can be calculated. You could also refer to the use of a displacement can to determine the ring's volume.

> The final part of the answer explains how the density value obtained tells you whether the material is gold or not – notice how the answer states that the ring *might be* gold, since you cannot say for definite as other materials may have this density.

When you structure your answer, make sure that you address the question in an order that allows you to deal with each of the points being asked for. Do not just list equations and facts. Communicate to the examiner that you understand how to find the density of the rings and how it will allow you to determine if the rings are real or fake based on the known value for the density of gold.

Now try this

A gas contains many particles moving with random motion in a container of a fixed volume.

Explain how the pressure of a gas can be increased by changing its volume or temperature.

Your answer should refer to energy, forces and the motion of the particles in the gas. **(6 marks)**

The structure of the atom

The atom is composed of protons, neutrons and electrons.

Structure of the atom

Atoms have a **nucleus** containing **protons** and **neutrons**. **Electrons** move around the nucleus of an atom. An atom has the same number of protons and electrons, so the **+** and **− charges** balance and the atom has no overall charge.

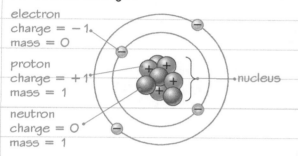

electron
charge = − 1
mass = 0

proton
charge = + 1
mass = 1

neutron
charge = 0
mass = 1

nucleus

The atom and the nucleus

1 All atoms have a **nucleus**. The **nucleus** is always **positively charged** as it contains **protons** which have a positive charge and neutrons which do not have a charge.

2 The **nucleus** contains more than **99%** of the **mass** of the atom.

3 The total number of **protons** in an atom's **nucleus** must be the same as the total number of **electrons** in the shells.

4 Electrons in atoms always orbit the **nucleus** and have a **negative charge**.

5 Atoms are always **neutral** because the positive charge from the **protons** cancels out the negative charge from the **electrons**.

6 The **nucleus** of an atom of an element may contain **different numbers of neutrons**.

The atom and the nucleus

The diameter of the atom is about 10^{-10} m in diameter. The diameter of the nucleus is much smaller at around 10^{-15} m. Diagrams to show atoms in textbooks are always incorrect in terms of their scale. In reality, if the nucleus on the left were the size shown here, the nearest electron would be at least 1000 m away.

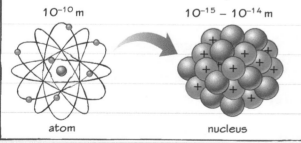

10^{-10} m $10^{-15} - 10^{-14}$ m

atom   nucleus

Moving between energy levels

An **electron** will move from a **lower to a higher orbit** if it **absorbs** electromagnetic radiation.

An **electron** will move from a **higher to a lower orbit** if it **emits** electromagnetic radiation.

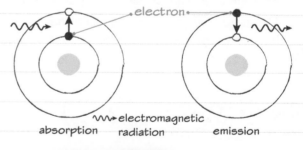

electron

absorption   electromagnetic radiation   emission

Worked example

An atom has diameter 4.8×10^{-10} m.
A nucleus has diameter 1.2×10^{-15} m.
How many nuclei would need to be placed side by side in a line to have the same length as the atom? **(3 marks)**

$(4.8 \times 10^{-10}$ m$) \div (1.2 \times 10^{-15}$ m$) = 4 \times 10^{5}$
or 400 000 nuclei.

Now try this

1 A poster shows a diagram of an atom that is not drawn to scale. The overall diameter of the atom on the poster is 60 cm. Calculate the diameter of the nucleus on the poster if it were properly drawn to scale. **(4 marks)**

2 Explain what happens when atoms
   (a) absorb radiation **(2 marks)**
   (b) emit radiation. **(2 marks)**

Maths skills When dividing values in standard form, remember that you need to
- divide the numbers at the front
- subtract the powers.

i.e. $(A \times 10^{x}) \div (B \times 10^{y}) = (A/B) \times 10^{(x-y)}$

Atoms, isotopes and ions

Particles can exist as neutrally charged atoms or as positively or negatively charged ions.

Atoms and isotopes

Atoms of a particular element always contain the **same number** of **protons** in their nucleus, but they may contain **different numbers** of **neutrons**. These atoms are called **isotopes** of the element.

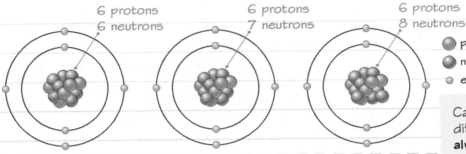

6 protons
6 neutrons

6 protons
7 neutrons

6 protons
8 neutrons

⬤ proton (atomic mass = 1)
⬤ neutron (atomic mass = 1)
○ electron (atomic mass = 0)

> Carbon atoms can contain different numbers of neutrons, but **always** contain 6 protons. If the number of protons changes, then the element will also change.

Forming positive ions

In an atom the number of electrons is equal to the number of protons. There is no net charge on the atom.

Atoms become positively charged particles called **positive ions** when they **lose electrons**. There are now more protons present in the nucleus than there are electrons in the shells.

Electrons can leave an atom by:

1 absorbing electromagnetic radiation of enough energy so that they can escape the pull of the nucleus.

The three types of electromagnetic radiation that have enough energy to do that are UV, X-rays and gamma-rays.

2 being hit by a particle such as an alpha particle or a beta particle.

electromagnetic radiation

Electron gets knocked off.

electron shells

alpha or beta particle

Electron gets knocked off.

Worked example

State the overall charge of
(a) an atom **(1 mark)**

neutral or 0

(b) a sodium atom that has lost an electron **(1 mark)**

+1

(c) an atom where an electron has moved from a higher to a lower orbit. **(1 mark)**

neutral or 0

> All atoms have a neutral overall charge. Positive ions are formed when an atom loses an electron.
>
> Atoms can also gain electrons. They become negative ions with an overall negative charge.

> No electron has been lost from the atom so there is no net change in the amount of charge present within the atom.

Now try this

 1 State what an isotope is. **(2 marks)**

2 Explain how ions are different from atoms. **(4 marks)**

 3 Describe how electromagnetic radiation can cause some atoms to become ions but not others. **(4 marks)**

Models of the atom

The **model of the atom** has changed over time, based on **evidence** of its structure which became available from **experiments**.

Plum pudding model

The discovery of the electron led to J. J. Thomson's model of the atom. He suggested the atom was like a 'plum pudding' with negatively charged 'electron plums' embedded in a uniform, positively charged 'dough' – a bit like the way currants look in a Christmas pudding. This model showed that both positive and negative charges existed in atoms and accounted for the atom being neutral.

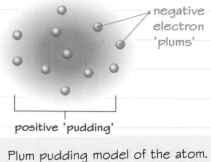

negative electron 'plums'

positive 'pudding'

Plum pudding model of the atom.

Rutherford's model

Rutherford proposed that the atom must contain a very **small, positively charged nucleus** which electrons orbit – a bit like planets orbiting the Sun.

Rutherford's hypothesis was proved to be correct by Geiger and Marsden, who fired alpha particles at gold film. Later experiments led to the idea that the positive charge of any nucleus could be subdivided into a whole number of smaller particles (protons), each particle having the same amount of positive charge.

About 20 years after Rutherford's model of the nuclear atom was accepted, James Chadwick's experiments showed that another neutrally charged particle, the neutron, was present in the nuclei of atoms.

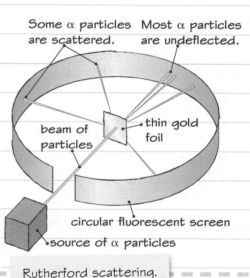

Some α particles are scattered.   Most α particles are undeflected.

beam of particles

thin gold foil

circular fluorescent screen

source of α particles

Rutherford scattering.

The Bohr model

Niels Bohr showed that **electrons** had to orbit a **positive nucleus** in well-defined **energy levels** or orbits, but could move between energy levels if they gained or lost energy.

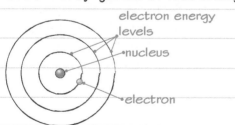

electron energy levels

nucleus

electron

The theoretical calculations of Bohr agreed with experimental observations, which is why his model was accepted.

Worked example

Describe how the plum pudding model and Rutherford's nuclear model are different.

(3 marks)

The plum pudding model describes the atom as a having a positive part in which negative electrons are embedded, whereas the nuclear model describes the atom as having a small, positive nucleus around which electrons orbit.

Now try this

1 Describe how Rutherford's work led to the conclusion that the atom had a small, positive nucleus.

(4 marks)

2 Describe how the plum pudding model was replaced by Rutherford's nuclear model, and how this was then replaced by the Bohr model.

(4 marks)

Radioactive decay

Unstable nuclei give out radiation to make themselves more stable. This random process is called radioactive decay.

Activity

Activity is the rate at which a source of unstable nuclei decays. Activity is measured in becquerels (Bq). If a source of radioactive nuclei is very unstable it will have a high activity, for example 1 000 000 Bq. This means that 1 000 000 nuclei are decaying each second. A more stable source of radioactive nuclei may have a much lower activity of only 20 Bq, meaning that only 20 unstable nuclei are decaying each second.

Activity-time graph

The activity of a radioactive source can be plotted against time. Over time, the activity decreases. This is because there are fewer and fewer unstable nuclei left to decay as unstable nuclei eventually turn into stable nuclei.

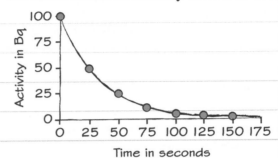

The activity of a radioactive source is often described in terms of its half-life (see page 42).

Changes to the nucleus

When a radioactive source decays, the changes to the nucleus depend on the type of particles that are emitted.

Type of radiation	Effect on the mass of the nucleus	Effect on the charge of the nucleus
alpha α	nuclear mass reduced by 4 [−4]	positive charge reduced by 2 [−2]
beta β	no change [0]	positive charge increased by 1 [+1]
gamma γ	no effect on either the mass or the charge of a nucleus	

Count rate and the Geiger–Müller tube

The Geiger–Müller (GM) tube is used to detect nuclear radiation. It is connected to a counter or ratemeter, which shows the count rate. The count rate is the number of alpha or beta particles or gamma-rays detected by a GM tube in a unit of time.

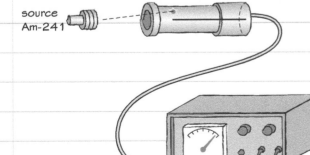

ratemeter

Worked example

A sample of radioactive material undergoes 5400 nuclear decays over a period of 1 minute. What is the activity of the source?   **(2 marks)**

activity = number of decays per second
= 5400 nuclear decays ÷ 60 s
= 90 decays per second or 90 Bq

Now try this

1 (a) Define the term activity.   **(2 marks)**
  (b) State the unit for activity.   **(1 mark)**
2 State what happens to the activity of a radioactive source over time.   **(1 mark)**
3 Describe what happens to the stability of a radioactive nucleus over time.   **(2 marks)**

Nuclear radiation

Alpha, **beta**, **gamma** and **neutron** radiation are **emitted** by **unstable nuclei**. The process is **random**, which means it is not possible to determine exactly **when** any nucleus will decay next.

Alpha, beta, gamma and neutron radiation

Some elements are **radioactive** because their nuclei are **unstable**. This means that they will undergo radioactive decay and change into other elements. Unstable nuclei will decay when alpha, beta, gamma or neutron radiation is emitted.

An **alpha particle** is a helium nucleus. It is composed of two protons and two neutrons.

It has a charge of +2 and is the heaviest of the particles emitted by unstable atoms. A **beta particle** is a high-speed electron. It has a charge of −1.

A **gamma-ray** is a form of high-energy electromagnetic radiation. It has no mass or charge.

A **neutron** has zero charge.

Properties of radiation

Alpha and beta particles and gamma-rays can collide with atoms, ionising them by causing them to lose electrons.

Neutrons:
- are not directly ionising
- have a very high penetrating power due to them having no charge and not interacting strongly with matter
- can travel through humans and buildings for long distances before being stopped.

① (α) Alpha particles:
- will travel around 5 cm in air
- very ionising
- can be stopped by a sheet of paper.

② (β) Beta particles:
- will travel a few metres in air
- moderately ionising
- can be stopped by aluminium 3-mm thick.

③ (γ) Gamma-rays:
- will travel a few kilometres in air
- weakly ionising
- need thick lead to stop them.

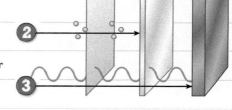

Worked example

Complete the table to show the properties of alpha, beta, gamma and neutron radiation. **(4 marks)**

Type of radiation emitted	Relative charge	Relative mass	Ionising power	Penetrating power
alpha, α (helium nucleus, two protons and two neutrons)	+2	4	heavily ionising	very low, only ~5 cm in air
beta, β (an electron from the nucleus)	−1	1/1840	weakly ionising	low, stopped by thin aluminium
neutron, n	0	1	not directly ionising	high
gamma, γ (waves)	0	0	not directly ionising	very high, stopped only by thick lead

Now try this

1 State the order of ionising power of nuclear radiation from least ionising to most ionising. **(1 mark)**

2 Radioactive decay is a random process. State what is meant by a random process. **(2 marks)**

3 Explain why alpha particles are not likely to be harmful if they are far away from a person, but would be harmful if they were swallowed. **(3 marks)**

Uses of nuclear radiation

The **uses** of alpha and beta particles and gamma-rays depend on their **properties**.

Uses of gamma-rays

Radiation is used in hospitals to:

- **kill cancer cells** – beams of gamma-rays can be directed at cancer cells to kill them.
- **sterilise surgical instruments** – gamma-rays can be used to sterilise plastic instruments which cannot be sterilised by heating.
- **diagnose cancer** – a **tracer** solution containing a radioactive isotope that emits gamma-rays is injected into the body and taken up by cells which are growing abnormally. The places in the body where the tracer collects are detected with a 'gamma camera'.
- **preserve food** – food irradiated with gamma-rays will last longer as microbes are killed by the high-energy gamma-rays. The food does not become radioactive.

Smoke alarms

Smoke alarms contain a source of **alpha particles**.

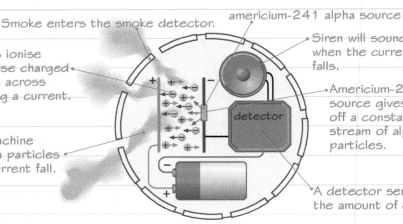

Smoke enters the smoke detector.

americium-241 alpha source

Siren will sound when the current falls.

Alpha particles ionise the air and these charged particles move across the gap forming a current.

Americium-241 source gives off a constant stream of alpha particles.

Smoke in the machine will absorb alpha particles and make the current fall.

A detector senses the amount of current.

Controlling paper thickness

If the paper is too thick, not as many beta particles get through.

The rollers press together harder to make the paper thinner or move apart to make it thicker.

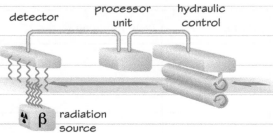

detector   processor unit   hydraulic control

β radiation source

Beta particles are used to control the thickness of paper.

Now try this

1 State **three** uses of ionising radiation. **(3 marks)**

2 Explain why the radiation in smoke alarms is not dangerous to people in homes. **(3 marks)**

3 Explain why a source of alpha particles is the best source of radiation to use in a smoke detector. **(3 marks)**

Nuclear equations

Unstable nuclei can undergo radioactive decay through the emission of alpha, beta or gamma radiation.

Alpha decay

In any nuclear decay, the total mass and charge of the nucleus are conserved – they are the same before and after the decay. So the masses and charges on each side of the equation must balance.

When uranium-238 undergoes alpha decay, mass and charge are conserved. Nuclei that have undergone radioactive decay also undergo a rearrangement of their protons and neutrons. This involves the loss of energy from the nucleus in the form of gamma radiation. The mass and charge of the gamma-ray must be zero for the equation to balance:

See page 38 for a summary of how radioactive decay changes the nucleus.

$$^{238}_{92}U \longrightarrow {}^{234}_{90}Th + {}^{4}_{2}\alpha + \gamma$$

uranium   thorium   alpha   gamma-
                              particle   ray

The emission of a gamma-ray after alpha decay does not change the mass number or atomic number of the nucleus – only energy is carried away, not mass or charge.

Beta decay

In β decay, a **neutron** in the nucleus of an unstable atom decays to become a **proton** and an **electron**. The proton stays within the nucleus, but the **electron**, which is the β **particle**, is emitted from the nucleus at high speed as a fast-moving electron.

$$n \longrightarrow p + e^-$$

The decay of **carbon-14** into **nitrogen-14** by the emission of a β particle is an example of β decay. The mass number does not change, but the proton number **increases** by 1.

$$^{14}_{6}C \longrightarrow {}^{14}_{7}N + {}^{0}_{-1}e$$

$^{0}_{-1}e$ is the emitted β particle.

Worked example

Explain the changes that take place during beta decay. **(3 marks)**

A neutron in the nucleus changes into a proton and a beta particle is emitted as a high-speed electron. The mass number does not change but the proton number increases by 1.

Although mass has been lost in the form of a beta particle, it is too small to affect the mass number, which does not change.

Worked example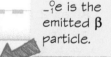

(a) An isotope of carbon undergoes β decay to form nitrogen-14. Balance the equation. **(2 marks)**

$$^{14}_{6}C \longrightarrow {}^{14}_{7}N + {}^{0}_{-1}e$$

(b) Radon-220 undergoes α decay to form an isotope of polonium. Balance the equation. **(2 marks)**

$$^{220}_{86}Rn \longrightarrow {}^{216}_{84}Po + {}^{4}_{2}He$$

$^{4}_{2}He$ is the emitted α particle.

Now try this

1 Describe the changes in mass and charge that occur during
   (a) alpha decay **(3 marks)**
   (b) beta decay. **(3 marks)**

2 Balance the following equation for the decay of caesium to barium by beta decay. **(3 marks)**

$$^{}_{55}Cs \longrightarrow {}^{137}Ra + {}^{}_{-1}e$$

3 Balance the following equation to show the decay of thorium to radium by alpha decay. **(2 marks)**

$$^{232}_{}Th \longrightarrow {}^{}_{88}Ra + {}^{4}_{2}He$$

Half-life

The activity of a radioactive source decreases over time according to the half-life of the source.

Unstable atoms

The activity of a source depends on how many **unstable** atoms there are in a sample, and on the particular isotope. As more and more atoms in a sample decay, there are fewer unstable ones left, so the activity decreases. The **half-life** of a radioactive isotope is the time it takes for **half** of the **unstable** atoms to **decay**. This is also the time for the activity to go down by half.

We cannot predict when a particular nucleus will decay – radioactive decay is a **random** process. But when there are very large numbers of nuclei, the half-life gives a good prediction of the proportion of nuclei that will decay in a given time.

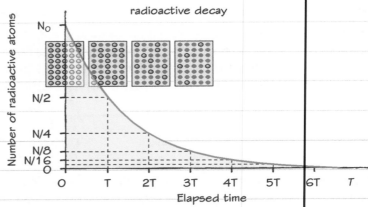

Radioactive decay and half-life

The number of radioactive nuclei present in a sample will halve after each successive half-life. After 1 half-life there will be 50% of the radioactive atoms left; after 2 half-lives there will be 25% of the radioactive atoms left, and so on.

Half-life example

The activity of a radioactive source is 240 Bq and its half-life is 6 hours.

After 1 half-life, the activity will halve to 120 Bq.

After 2 half-lives it will halve again to 60 Bq.

After 3 half-lives it will halve again to 30 Bq.

After 4 half-lives (one day) it will be 15 Bq.

As the activity of a radioactive source decreases, the gradient of the graph will get less and less steep.

Worked example

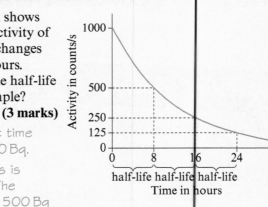

The graph shows how the activity of a sample changes over 24 hours. What is the half-life of the sample? **(3 marks)**

Activity at time 0 = 1000 Bq.

Half of this is 500 Bq. The activity is 500 Bq at 8 hours.

The half-life is 8 hours.

Now try this

1 The activity of a source is 120 Bq. Four hours later it is found to be 30 Bq. Calculate the half-life of the source. **(2 marks)**

2 The graph shows how the activity of a source from a radioactive sample changes over time. Use the graph to work out the half-life of the sample. **(2 marks)**

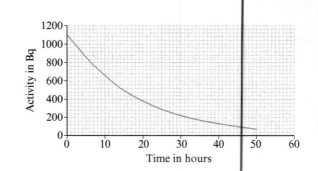

Contamination and irradiation

You may be exposed to the effects of radioactive materials by being **irradiated** or **contaminated**.

Irradiation

Irradiation is ionising radiation from an external radioactive source travelling to the body – it is not breathed in, eaten or drunk.

Irradiation does not refer to non-harmful rays from televisions, light bulbs or other non-ionising sources.

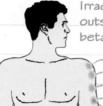

Alpha particles are unlikely to be harmful outside the body as they have a very short range in air (5 cm) and are unlikely to reach a person.

Irradiation is the exposure of a person to ionising radiation from outside the body. This could be in the form of harmful gamma-rays, beta particles or X-rays.

When ionising radiation reaches the body, cells may be damaged or killed, but you will not become radioactive.

Contamination

Radioactive **contamination** is the unwanted presence of radioactive material on or inside other materials or human bodies. The hazard posed by the contamination depends on the nature of the decay of the contaminating atoms.

External contamination occurs when radioactive materials **come into contact with a person's hair, skin or clothing.**

Internal contamination occurs when **a radioactive source is eaten or drunk.** Some nuts, plants, fruits and alcoholic drinks have low levels of radioactivity. This is due to the radioactive minerals that they are exposed to during their growth or manufacture.

Worked example

State what type of contamination the following examples are describing:
(a) eating radioactive strontium-90 that is found in some foods **(1 mark)**
internal contamination
(b) being exposed to cosmic rays from the Sun **(1 mark)**
irradiation
(c) having an X-ray to find if a bone is broken **(1 mark)**
irradiation
(d) radioactive dust comes into contact with the skin. **(1 mark)**
external contamination.

Remember that, with contamination, the radioactive source comes into contact with the skin or is taken into the body. This can be through the mouth or nose, or through a cut in the skin. With irradiation, the source does not come into contact with the skin.

Now try this

1 Describe the difference between irradiation and contamination. **(2 marks)**

2 Describe how background radiation is a mixture of contamination and irradiation. **(2 marks)**

Hazards of radiation

Ionising radiation can knock electrons out of atoms, turning the atoms into **ions**. This can be very **harmful** to humans.

Precautions and safety

People who come into contact with ionising radiation need to be protected. They are protected by:

1 **limiting the time of exposure** – keep the time that a person needs to be in contact with the ionising radiation as **low** as possible.

2 **wearing protective clothing** – wearing a **lead apron** will **absorb** much of the ionising radiation.

3 **increasing the distance from the person to the radioactive source** – the **further** a person is from the ionising radiation, the **less damage** it will do.

To determine how much radiation a person has been exposed to, a film badge may be worn.

The **greater the half-life** of an ionising source, the **longer** it will remain **dangerous**.

Precautions

People using radioactive material take precautions to make sure that they stay safe.

radioactive source

The radioactive source is being moved using tongs to keep it as far away from the person's hand as possible. The source is always kept pointing away from people.

Dangers to the body

A source of alpha particles with a high activity will be most hazardous inside the human body. Gamma-rays are less dangerous inside the body, because they can pass out of the body without causing much harm to cells.

Radiation studies

It is important that the findings of studies into the effects of nuclear radiation on the body are published to inform people of the impact of radiation on their bodies. Scientists also need to share their findings with others in the scientific community so that they can test these claims. This is called peer review.

Worked example

Describe two precautions taken by dentists and dental nurses to reduce their exposure to ionising radiation while taking an X-ray. **(2 marks)**

1. They go out of the room in which the X-ray is taking place.
2. They keep the X-ray pulse as short as possible. (This also minimises the patient's exposure.)

The amount of energy that the human body is exposed to from a radioactive source is referred to as the **dose**. The dose needs to be big enough to obtain the X-ray image, but low enough to be safe for the patient and the dentist.

Now try this

1 Describe **three** precautions that can be taken to avoid unnecessary exposure to radiation.   **(3 marks)**

2 Explain why peer review is important in the scientific community.   **(2 marks)**

3 Suggest why ionising radiation is more dangerous than non-ionising radiation.   **(3 marks)**

Background radiation

Low levels of **radiation** are present around you all the time. This radiation is both **natural** and **man-made** and is called **background radiation**.

Background radiation

We are always exposed to ionising radiation. This is called **background radiation**. This radiation comes from different sources, as shown in the pie chart.

Radon is a radioactive gas that is produced when **uranium** in rocks decays. Radon decays by emitting an alpha particle. The radon can build up in houses and other buildings. The amount of radon gas varies from place to place, because it depends on the type of rock in the area.

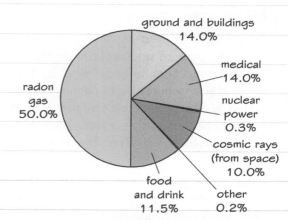

ground and buildings 14.0%
medical 14.0%
nuclear power 0.3%
cosmic rays (from space) 10.0%
other 0.2%
food and drink 11.5%
radon gas 50.0%

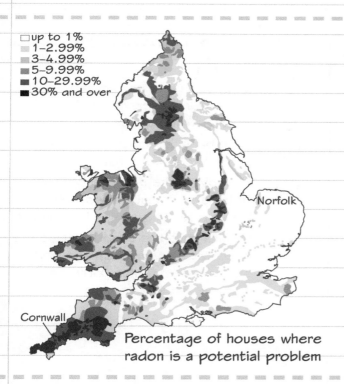

- ☐ up to 1%
- ☐ 1–2.99%
- ☐ 3–4.99%
- ☐ 5–9.99%
- ☐ 10–29.99%
- ☐ 30% and over

Norfolk

Cornwall

Percentage of houses where radon is a potential problem

Worked example

Give two examples of background radiation that are:

(a) naturally occurring   **(2 marks)**

cosmic rays and radioactivity from the ground

(b) from human activities.   **(2 marks)**

nuclear power and medical, e.g. hospitals

Naturally occurring background radiation comes from the environment around you such as the **soil**, **rocks**, **food**, **drink** and **cosmic rays** from outer space.

The artificial sources from human activities come from nuclear power stations, fallout from nuclear weapons testing and nuclear accidents and from departments in medical settings, such as hospitals, where radioactive materials are made and used.

Radiation dose

Radiation dose is measured in units called sieverts (Sv) or millisieverts (mSv); 1000 mSv = 1 Sv. The dose of the background radiation is very low – around 0.000 003 Sv or 0.003 mSv per hour. A radiation dose of 0.1 Sv will lead to death.

Half-lives and hazards

Radioactive isotopes have a very wide range of half-lives, ranging from fractions of a second to many millions of years. The threat to human health is greater if the half-life is long and the dose to which we are exposed is high – because living cells will be exposed to dangerous radiation for a longer amount of time. The background radiation dose is very low, so the risk to human health is also low.

Now try this

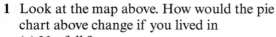

1 Look at the map above. How would the pie chart above change if you lived in
(a) Norfolk?
(b) Cornwall?   **(2 marks)**

2 Explain why radon is more dangerous inside the body than outside the body.   **(3 marks)**

Medical uses

Nuclear radiation can be used in medicine for the exploration of organs and the control or destruction of unwanted tissue.

Medical tracers

Properties of medical tracers:

- An isotope of an element or part of a compound that is absorbed by the body.
- Usually an emitter of gamma-rays.
- Half-life long enough to give a useful image, but short enough so that its nuclei have mostly decayed after the image has been taken.

Medical tracers are substances that are used in **biological** processes in the body and contain a **radioisotope**.

The patient can **eat** or **drink** this substance, or it can be **injected** into the body.

The **ionising radiation** emitted by the tracer can be **detected** and the biological process **monitored**. Doctors can diagnose the nature and location of any health problems.

For example, **fluorodeoxyglucose (FDG)** is a radioactive form of glucose that is commonly used as a tracer. In the blood FDG travels to the tissues that use glucose. When part of the brain is affected, **less radioactivity** is detected because glucose is not being used.

Destroying unwanted tissue internally

Cancer tumours can be treated internally by using a radioactive source that is inside the patient. The source enters the patient by:

1. **injecting** the radioisotope into the patient

2. the patient **eating** or **drinking** something that contains the radioisotope in solid or liquid form.

Radioactive implants are used to destroy cancer cells in some tumours. Beta- or gamma-emitting isotopes are used in the form of small seeds or tiny rods. Radioisotopes are used with half-lives long enough to irradiate the tumour over a given time, but short enough to limit the dose to the patient.

The radioactive element iodine-131 is used to treat thyroid cancer. It is swallowed in a capsule. The iodine is taken up by the thyroid gland but not by other parts of the body. This means that the ionising radiation is likely to kill the thyroid cancer without affecting healthy cells surrounding it.

Destroying unwanted tissue externally

1. Several beams of gamma-rays are fired, from different positions, towards the cancer.

2. Each beam is not energetic enough to kill the tumour, but damages it.

3. By moving the beam, the amount of ionising radiation received by the surrounding tissue is reduced.

4. Gamma-rays are used because they penetrate deeper into the body than alpha and beta particles from an external source.

source of gamma-rays

gamma-rays

target

Worked example

Describe how gamma-rays can be used in nuclear medicine. **(2 marks)**

Gamma-rays can be used to form images of the internal workings of the body and they can also be used to destroy or control cancer cells.

Don't confuse the uses – gamma-rays can be used effectively to do both of these jobs.

Now try this

 1 Explain why several low-energy gamma-ray beams are used instead of a single high-energy beam when treating cancer with gamma-rays from an external source. **(4 marks)**

 2 Describe why some radioisotopes would not be suitable for use as medical tracers. **(3 marks)**

Nuclear fission

The fission of uranium or plutonium nuclei results in the **release of large quantities of energy**, which is then used to **heat water** in power stations.

Nuclear fission

In a **fission reaction**, a large unstable nucleus splits into two smaller ones. For example, a **uranium-235** nucleus splits up when it absorbs a **neutron**. The fission of uranium-235 produces two **daughter nuclei** that are roughly the same size, two or more neutrons, and also releases energy. The daughter nuclei are also radioactive.

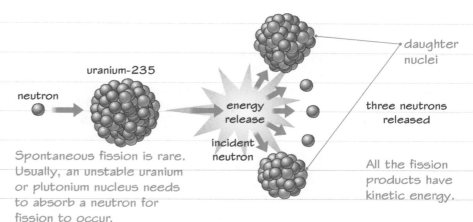

Spontaneous fission is rare. Usually, an unstable uranium or plutonium nucleus needs to absorb a neutron for fission to occur.

All the fission products have kinetic energy.

Controlled chain reactions

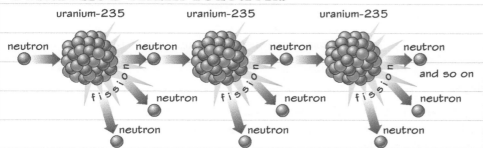

Two of the neutrons are absorbed by other materials. Only one neutron from each fission can cause other fission. This is a **controlled chain reaction**.

Chain reactions

The neutrons released by the fission of ^{235}U may be absorbed by other nuclei. Each of these nuclei may undergo fission, and produce even more neutrons. This is called a **chain reaction**. If a chain reaction is not controlled there will be a nuclear explosion. Nuclear reactors make use of **controlled** chain reactions.

Worked example

Describe how a chain reaction can be controlled.

(3 marks)

A chain reaction can be controlled by using a different material to absorb some of the neutrons. This slows the reaction down because there are fewer neutrons to cause more nuclei to undergo fission.

Now try this

1 Describe what happens in the fission of uranium-235.   **(3 marks)**

2 Describe the difference between a chain reaction and a controlled chain reaction.   **(4 marks)**

3 Explain why:
    (a) neutrons in a nuclear reaction need to be slow moving   **(2 marks)**
    (b) only one neutron should be absorbed by a uranium-235 nucleus.   **(2 marks)**

Nuclear fusion

Nuclear fusion involves the **joining of smaller nuclei** to form **larger nuclei**. Obtaining a continuous supply of energy from nuclear fusion is **more difficult** than obtaining energy from nuclear fission.

Nuclear fusion

Nuclear **fusion** happens when small nuclei join to form larger ones. Like all nuclear reactions, fusion reactions **release energy**. Some of the mass is converted into energy.

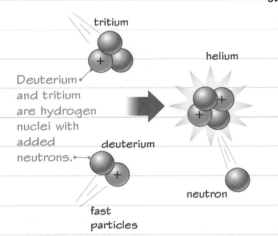

Deuterium and tritium are hydrogen nuclei with added neutrons.

tritium

helium

deuterium

neutron

fast particles

Fusion and stars

During the stable period of a star's life, vast quantities of hydrogen nuclei are converted to helium nuclei by nuclear fusion. This is the source of energy for stars.

Over time, heavier elements are formed and the star will eventually die. This will take our Sun billions of years. One of the typical reactions that takes place in the Sun is:

$$^2_1H + ^3_1H \longrightarrow ^4_2He + ^1_0n + \text{energy}$$

The mass of the products is slightly less than the mass of the reactants – this mass difference is released as energy in the form of thermal energy.

This reaction takes place under very high pressure and temperature in stars.

Difficulties of fusion

Nuclei need to get very close to each other before fusion can happen. Under normal conditions the positive charges on nuclei repel each other. This is called **electrostatic repulsion**. Only at very high temperatures and pressures are the nuclei moving fast enough for them to overcome this electrostatic repulsion.

The very high temperatures and pressures needed are very difficult to produce in a fusion power station. All the experimental fusion reactors built so far have used more energy than they have produced!

Worked example

Describe the similarities and differences between nuclear fusion and nuclear fission. **(3 marks)**

In nuclear fusion hydrogen nuclei fuse to produce helium nuclei whereas in nuclear fission uranium-235 splits into two smaller nuclei and two or three neutrons.

Nuclear fusion requires very high temperatures and pressures whereas nuclear fission requires a slow-moving neutron to be absorbed.

Both processes release large quantities of energy.

Fusion can occur in the Sun and other stars because the enormous temperatures and pressures allow the charged nuclei to overcome the repulsive electrostatic forces between them.

Now try this

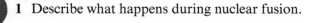

1 Describe what happens during nuclear fusion. **(3 marks)**

2 Describe how the processes of fusion and fission release energy. **(4 marks)**

Extended response – Radioactivity

There will be at least one 6-mark question on your exam paper. For these questions, you will need to think scientifically and structure your answer logically, showing how the points you make are related to each other. You can revise the topics for this question, which is about **radioactivity**, on pages 35–48.

Worked example

Some types of cancer can be treated by using a radioactive material from inside the body, whereas other cancers are treated by using a radioactive source outside the body.

Explain how cancer can be treated in both cases.

Your answer should refer to examples of suitable isotopes, the radiation emitted and the half-life of these isotopes. **(6 marks)**

Internal radiation therapy involves the placing of a radioactive source inside the patient. Alternatively, the radioisotope can be injected, swallowed or enter the body via an intravenous drip. The radioisotope then travels through the body, locating and killing cancer cells. For radioactive materials that are used internally to treat cancer, the half-life of the source is low – it could be a few hours, days or weeks depending on the nature of the cancer being treated. One example is iodine-131, which has a half-life of 8 days and is used to treat thyroid cancer. It is a beta emitter, although alpha emitters are also used internally as these only need to travel short distances. The half-life of the source needs to be long enough to treat the cancer but not so long as to cause long-term harm to the patient.

When treating a tumour externally, weak gamma-rays are fired from different positions around the body so as to focus the gamma-rays on the cancer tumour but not to cause too much damage to the healthy cells surrounding the tumour. The gamma-rays come from an external source which should have a long half-life so that it does not need to be constantly replaced. An example of such a source is cobalt-60, which has a half-life of between 5 and 6 years.

Command word: Explain

When you are asked to **explain** something, it is not enough just to state or describe it. Your answer **must** contain some reasoning or justification of the points you make. Your explanation **can** include mathematical explanations, if calculations are needed.

 The answer starts by explaining how a cancer tumour can be targeted from inside the body. The methods used to get the material into the body are explained, as is an example of a suitable isotope, a typical half-life value and suitable types of radioactive particle that are emitted.

 The second part of the answer refers to how cancer can be treated from an external source. The reason for the long half-life and a suitable gamma source are given.

Internal vs external sources of radiotherapy

External sources of radiotherapy tend to use gamma-rays for irradiating the patient. The patient does not become radioactive after treatment. However, a patient does become radioactive if they are treated internally as they have been contaminated with radioactive material which can emit particles that will leave the body.

Now try this

Radioactive material is used in smoke alarms. Explain the characteristics of the radioactive material used in smoke alarms. Your answer should refer to suitable and unsuitable radioactive materials for this purpose.

(6 marks)

Scalars and vectors

All physical quantities can be described as either a scalar or a vector quantity.

Scalar quantities

Scalar quantities have a size or a magnitude but no specific direction.

Examples include:
- mass
- speed
- distance
- energy
- temperature.

Vector quantities

Vector quantities have a size or magnitude and a specific direction.

Examples include:
- force or weight
- velocity
- displacement
- acceleration
- momentum.

Speed and velocity

The girl is running to the right so she has a velocity of 8 m/s to the right.

8 m/s

The boy and girl are running at different speeds.

4 m/s

The boy is running to the left so he has a velocity of 4 m/s to the left.

The length of an arrow shows the size of the vector. As the girl is running at twice the speed of the boy, her arrow is twice as long. The direction of movement is also shown by the arrows.

Speed has a size but velocity has a size AND a direction.

Velocity is speed in a stated direction.

If we take 'to the right' as the positive direction, then the girl has a velocity of +8 m/s and the boy has a velocity of −4 m/s.

Worked example

(a) Describe the difference between a scalar and a vector. **(2 marks)**

A scalar has a size, whereas a vector has a size and a specific direction.

(b) Describe an example that shows the difference between a scalar and a vector. **(2 marks)**

Speed is a scalar quantity and may have a value of 5 m/s. Velocity may also have a value of 5 m/s but a direction of north.

All vector quantities can be given positive and negative values to show their direction. Examples include:

1 A force of +4 N may be balanced by a force acting in the opposite direction of −4 N.

2 A car that accelerates at a rate of +2 m/s² could decelerate at −2 m/s².

3 If a distance walked to the right of 20 m is a displacement of +20 m, then the same distance walked to the left from the same starting point is a displacement of −20 m.

Now try this

1 (a) Which of these quantities is a scalar? **(1 mark)**

☐ velocity   ☐ acceleration   ☐ mass   ☐ weight

(b) Which of these quantities is a vector? **(1 mark)**

☐ temperature   ☐ energy   ☐ speed   ☐ electric field

2 A boy has a speed of 4 m/s when running. State his (a) speed and (b) velocity when he is running in the opposite direction. **(2 marks)**

3 Describe why a satellite can be said to be moving at a constant speed but not at a constant velocity. **(3 marks)**

Interacting forces

A force is a push or pull that acts on an object due to the interaction with another object. Pairs of forces can interact **at a distance** or by **direct contact**.

Non-contact forces

Forces can be exerted between objects without them being in contact with one another. There are three **non-contact forces** that you need to know about.

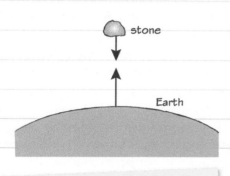
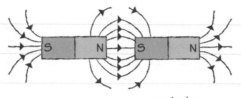
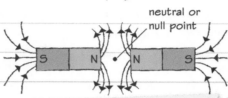
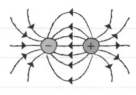
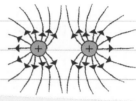

A gravitational force acts between all masses. It is always attractive.

A magnetic force acts between magnetic poles. Unlike poles attract and like poles repel.

Charges exert electrostatic forces on each other at a distance. Unlike charges attract and like charges repel.

Contact forces

Forces can be exerted between objects due to them being in contact. In each case there is an interaction pair of forces that act in opposite directions. The forces can be represented by vectors.

The **normal contact force** acts upwards in opposition to the weight of the object. The interaction pair is the force of the ground on the box and the force of the box on the ground.

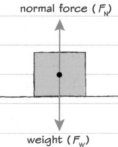
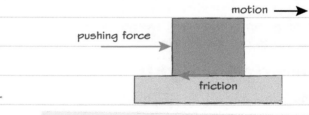

The **force of friction** acts in opposition to the pushing force that is trying to change its motion. Friction always acts to slow a moving object down. The interaction pair is the force of the object on the surface and the force of the surface on the object.

Other examples of contact forces include air resistance, tension and drag.

Worked example

An archer fires an arrow from a bow. Describe the contact and non-contact forces involved in firing the arrow. **(2 marks)**

Contact forces include the normal force acting on the arrow, friction as it moves through the air and the tension in the string. Non-contact forces include gravity once it has been released.

Now try this

1 State how gravity is different from magnetism and the electrostatic force. **(1 mark)**

2 State how the forces of friction and drag are similar. **(1 mark)**

3 Describe the contact and non-contact forces acting on a moving ship. **(3 marks)**

Gravity, weight and mass

It is important that you understand the difference between weight and mass. These words are often used interchangeably but are actually different things.

Weight

Weight is the **force** that a body experiences due to its mass and the size of the gravitational field that it is in.

Weight is a **vector** quantity and is measured in **newtons** (N).

The weight of a body on the surface of the Earth acts inwards towards the Earth's centre.

The weight of a body can be assumed to act downwards through a single point called its centre of mass.

Connection between mass and weight

To find the weight of an object, use the equation:

$$\frac{\text{weight}}{\text{in N}} = \frac{\text{mass}}{\text{in kg}} \times \frac{\text{gravitational field strength}}{\text{in N/kg}}$$

$$W = m\,g$$

The weight of an object is directly proportional to the value of g, so a mass will weigh more on Earth than it does on the Moon.

LEARN IT!
IT'S NOT ON THE EQUATIONS LIST

Measuring weight

Weight is measured using a calibrated spring balance (a newtonmeter).

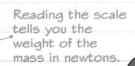

Reading the scale tells you the weight of the mass in newtons.

The greater the mass attached, the more weight it will experience due to gravity and the more the spring will stretch.

A 2-kg mass has twice the weight on Earth as a 1-kg mass, so the extension of the spring will be twice as big.

Mass

Mass is a measure of the **amount of matter** that is contained within a three-dimensional space.

Mass is a **scalar** quantity and is measured in **kilograms** (kg).

The mass of a body is not affected by the size of the gravitational field that it is in.

Weight and mass are directly proportional to each other. If you double the mass of an object on Earth, you will double the weight that it experiences due to gravity. You can use the symbol for proportionality, $\propto$:

weight $\propto$ mass

Gravitational field strength

The units of gravitational field strength are newtons per kilogram (N/kg), but it can also be given as m/s^2.

Astronomical body	Value for g in N/kg
Earth	10
Moon	1.6
Jupiter	26
Neptune	13.3
Mercury	3.6
Mars	3.75
neutron star	10^{12}

Worked example

An astronaut has a mass of 58 kg on Earth. State the astronaut's mass and weight:

(a) on the surface of the Moon (3 marks)

Mass does not change so it is still 58 kg.
weight = 58 kg × 1.6 N/kg = 92.8 N

(b) on the surface of Jupiter. (3 marks)

Mass does not change, so it is still 58 kg.
weight = 58 kg × 26 N/kg = 1508 N

Now try this

1 An astronaut has a mass of 76 kg on Earth. Calculate the astronaut's mass and weight:
   (a) on the surface of Mars   **(3 marks)**
   (b) on the surface of Neptune.   **(3 marks)**

2 Calculate the value for g on the surface of a planet where a mass of 18 kg experiences a weight of 54 N.   **(3 marks)**

Resultant forces

Resultant forces determine whether a body will be **stationary**, moving at a **constant speed** or **accelerating**.

Resultant forces

Forces are **vectors**, so they have a **size** and a **direction**. Both of these need to be taken into consideration when finding the resultant force.

The resultant force is the single force that would have the same effect as all of the other forces acting on the object. There can be many of these, but they always simplify to just one resultant force.

A resultant force of zero means that a body is either stationary or moving at a constant speed.

Forces acting in the same direction are added.

Forces acting in opposite directions are subtracted.

Worked example

The forces acting on a moving car are shown below. The car is moving to the right. Describe the motion of the car. **(3 marks)**

200 N drag

200 N forward force from the engine

The car will move at a constant speed to the right. There is no resultant force acting on the car, so it will not accelerate.

A resultant force is needed for a body to accelerate. A moving body will travel at a constant speed if the forces on it are balanced and the resultant force is zero.

Worked example

A ball is dropped from the top of a cliff and falls as shown. Describe the motion of the ball. **(3 marks)**

drag force

mg

The weight of the ball acting downwards is greater than the force of drag acting upwards. This means that there is a resultant force acting downwards on the ball, so the ball will accelerate downwards, towards the ground.

Now try this

1 Draw a diagram to show how two forces of 20 N can have a resultant force of
   (a) 40 N upwards **(1 mark)**
   (b) 0 N. **(1 mark)**
2 Describe the motion of a body that has a resultant force of 8 N acting on it towards the ground. **(2 marks)**
3 Describe the motion of a tennis ball that is thrown vertically upwards. **(3 marks)**

Work and energy

The work done by a force is the same as the energy transferred. You need to know how to calculate the work done or the energy transferred when a force moves a body.

Work done

When a force causes an object to move through a distance, work is done on the object. A force does work on an object when the force causes a displacement of the object. If a force of 1 N acts on a body and displaces it by 1 m then 1 J of work is done. This means that 1 Nm is equal to 1 J.

1 joule = 1 newton-metre.

Work done and energy

Work done is the amount of energy transferred, and is measured in **joules (J)**.

The work done by a force is calculated using this formula:

$$\text{work done in J} = \text{force in N} \times \text{distance moved in the direction of the force in m}$$

$$W = F\,s$$

LEARN IT!
IT'S NOT ON THE EQUATIONS LIST

You can measure work done by recording the size of the force and the distance moved in the direction of the force. Multiply these values together to find the value for work done.

Work done moving a body horizontally

Work, W, is done when a force, F, moves a body through a horizontal distance, s.

Work done against the frictional forces acting on the object will lead to a rise in temperature of the object. The greater the amount of friction, the more work has to be done to move the body through the same distance.

Work done when a body is lifted

When a body is lifted, work is done and there is an increase in the body's gravitational potential energy. The work done, or the increase in the gravitational potential energy (g.p.e.) store, is calculated using $W = F\,s$ or $E_p = m\,g\,h$

Worked example

Dan uses a force of 100 N to push a box across the floor. He pushes it for 3 m. Calculate the work done. **(3 marks)**

work done = 100 N × 3 m = 300 J

Worked example

Calculate how much work is done when a 20 kg mass is lifted through a height of 15 m.

work done = increase in the E_p store
= 20 kg × 10 N/kg × 15 m = 3000 J

Now try this

 1 Calculate how much work is done when 350 N pushes an object through 30 m along the floor. **(3 marks)**

 2 Calculate the force required to move a body a horizontal distance of 300 m when 360 000 J of work is done. **(3 marks)**

  3 Calculate the work done when a mass of 25 kg is raised through a vertical height of 40 m on Earth. **(3 marks)**

Forces and elasticity

The deformation of a material may be described as being **elastic** or **inelastic** and **requires more than one force.**

Bending, stretching and compressing

 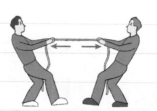 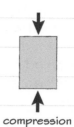

compression

Bending requires two forces, one acting clockwise and one acting anticlockwise.

Stretching requires two forces of tension, acting away from each other.

Compression involves two equal forces acting towards each other.

Elastic deformation

Elastic deformation means that a material will return to its original shape when the deforming force is removed.

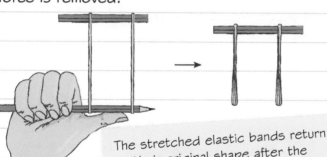

The stretched elastic bands return to their original shape after the deforming force is removed. They have undergone elastic deformation.

Inelastic deformation

Inelastic deformation means that a material will not return to its original shape when the deforming force is removed.

before   after

This spring has not returned to its original shape after being deformed, so it has undergone inelastic deformation.

Worked example

Describe what this graph shows for a spring that has been stretched. **(3 marks)**

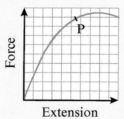

Force / Extension, point P

Initially, the extension is directly proportional to the force applied, so the behaviour of the spring is elastic for smaller forces.

Point P is the limit of proportionality. For forces applied after this, the relationship is no longer linear and the spring will not return to its original shape – it will exhibit inelastic deformation.

Now try this

1 Describe the types of forces that cause
   (a) stretching **(2 marks)**
   (b) compression. **(2 marks)**

2 Give examples of materials that exhibit
   (a) elastic deformation **(2 marks)**
   (b) inelastic deformation. **(2 marks)**
3 Describe the difference between elastic and inelastic deformation. **(2 marks)**

Force and extension

Forces can lead to the **deformation** of **elastic** objects, resulting in **energy** being stored.

Elastic distortion

A force applied to a spring can make it undergo linear elastic deformation. The equation that describes this is:

$$\text{force exerted on a spring in N} = \text{spring constant in N/m} \times \text{extension in m}$$

$$F = ke$$

LEARN IT!
IT'S NOT ON THE EQUATIONS LIST

You can calculate the work done in stretching or compressing a spring using the equation:

$$\text{elastic potential energy in J} = 0.5 \times \text{spring constant in N/m} \times (\text{extension})^2 \text{ in m}^2$$

$$E_e = \tfrac{1}{2}ke^2$$

Force and linear extension

For elastic distortion, **extension** is **directly proportional** to the **force** exerted, **up to the limit of proportionality**. The work done on the spring and the elastic potential energy stored are equal.

The extension is the amount the spring stretches.

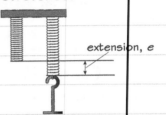

extension, e

Worked example

A spring is deformed elastically. It increases its length by 25 cm when a total weight of 12 N is added.

Calculate

(a) the spring constant of the spring   **(3 marks)**

$$k = \frac{F}{e} = \frac{12\,\text{N}}{0.25\,\text{m}} = 48\,\text{N/m}$$

(b) the total energy stored in the spring. **(4 marks)**

energy stored = work done

$$E = \tfrac{1}{2}k e^2$$
$$= \tfrac{1}{2} \times 48\,\text{N/m} \times (0.25\,\text{m})^2$$
$$= 1.5\,\text{J}$$

When calculating the spring constant, work done or energy stored, ensure that force is in N and extension is in m.

Always use the extension. You may need to calculate this:

$$\text{extension} = \frac{\text{total stretched length}}{} - \text{original length}$$

Force–extension graph

The gradient tells you the value of the spring constant, k. This is only true when the spring is showing elastic behaviour, i.e. when the line is straight.

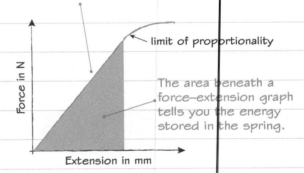

limit of proportionality

The area beneath a force–extension graph tells you the energy stored in the spring.

Force in N (vertical axis)
Extension in mm (horizontal axis)

The area under the graph is the area of a triangle $= \tfrac{1}{2}Fe$

The force is given by the equation $F = ke$

Substituting this into the equation gives

$$E_e = \tfrac{1}{2}(ke)e = \tfrac{1}{2}ke^2$$

Now try this

1 (a) Calculate the force that is required to extend a spring of spring constant 30 N/m by 20 cm.   **(3 marks)**
   (b) Calculate how much work is done on the spring under these conditions.   **(3 marks)**
2 Explain how the stiffness of a spring is related to its spring constant.   **(3 marks)**
3 Describe what happens to a spring for it to start displaying inelastic deformation.   **(3 marks)**

56

Force and extension

Practical skills In this investigation you are going to investigate the relationship between the force and extension of a spring.

Required practical

Aim

to investigate the relationship between the weight hung from a spring and the extension of the spring

> Wear eye protection when taking readings. A stretched spring stores a lot of elastic energy and this could damage your eyes if released.

Apparatus

spring, ruler, pointer, weights, retort stand, bosses and clamps

Method

Arrange the apparatus as shown. Use the ruler to measure the length of the unstretched spring. Add masses or weights and measure the position of the spring each time, so that the extension can be determined. Collect enough values to plot a graph of extension against force.

> When taking readings of the extension, read the values on the ruler at eye level to avoid parallax errors.

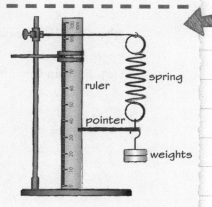

Weight and mass

Weight is a force, not a mass. A mass of 100 g is equivalent to a weight or force of 1 N.

Extension is equal to

new length − original length
in m   in m

The inverse of the gradient of an extension–force graph gives you the spring constant.

Results

Use your results to plot a graph of extension on the *y*-axis against weight on the *x*-axis. You can then determine the weight of a mystery object by using the extension of the spring when you hang the object from it on this graph.

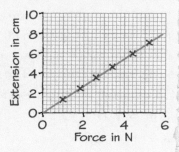

Maths skills You will need to convert extension values from mm to m before you can calculate an energy value, and state the result in joules, J. Forces also need to be stated in N, so any mass values recorded need to be converted from g to N.

Conclusion

There is a linear relationship between the extension of a spring and the weight applied. The extension of the spring will be directly proportional to the weight provided that the limit of proportionality is not exceeded.

Now try this

1 Describe how the results that you would obtain would differ for springs with different spring constant values.   **(4 marks)**
2 Describe what would happen if the investigation involved you adding weights so that the limit of proportionality of the spring was exceeded.   **(4 marks)**
3 Suggest whether the spring constant can be calculated for springs that are being compressed.   **(3 marks)**

Moments

Forces that act at a **distance** from a **pivot** can cause a **turning effect** or rotation. This is known as a **moment**.

Moments

The size of the moment, or turning effect, is given by the equation:

$$\begin{array}{c} \text{moment} \\ \text{in newton-} \\ \text{metres, Nm} \end{array} = \begin{array}{c} \text{force} \\ \text{in N} \end{array} \times \begin{array}{c} \text{distance normal} \\ \text{to the direction of} \\ \text{the force in m} \end{array}$$

$$M = F\,d$$

LEARN IT!
IT'S NOT ON THE EQUATIONS LIST

The distance must be measured from the pivot normal (at right angles, or **perpendicular**) to the direction of the force. The pivot is the point about which the object rotates.

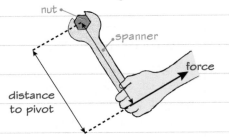

Worked example

Two children are sitting on a seesaw.

(a) Calculate the anticlockwise moment.

(2 marks)

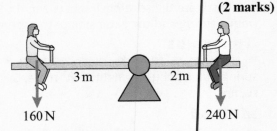

$160\,N \times 3\,m = 480\,Nm$

(b) Calculate the clockwise moment. **(2 marks)**

$240\,N \times 2\,m = 480\,Nm$

(c) Explain why the seesaw doesn't move.

(2 marks)

The anticlockwise and clockwise moments about the pivot are equal so the seesaw is balanced and does not move.

The principle of moments

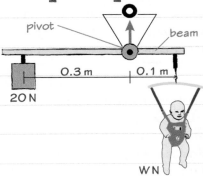

$$\begin{array}{c} \text{sum of the} \\ \text{clockwise moments} \end{array} = \begin{array}{c} \text{sum of the} \\ \text{anticlockwise moments} \end{array}$$

LEARN IT!
IT'S NOT ON THE EQUATIONS LIST

for rotational forces in equilibrium.

The diagram shows a common arrangement for weighing fruit and vegetables, as well as babies. The beam is balanced so:

anticlockwise moment = clockwise moment

$20\,N \times 0.3\,m = W\,N \times 0.1\,m$

$W = 6\,Nm/0.1\,m = 60\,N$

The weight of the bar has been ignored in this calculation.

Worked example

Ailsa and Ben are sitting on a seesaw. The seesaw is balanced. Work out Ben's weight, x.

As the seesaw is balanced:
clockwise moment = anticlockwise moment

Anticlockwise moment = 400 N × 4 m = 1600 Nm

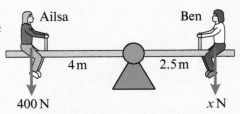

Clockwise moment = 1600 Nm = x N × 2.5 m

So $x = 1600 \div 2.5 = 640\,N$

Ben's weight is 640 N

Now try this

A uniform seesaw of length 3 m is pivoted at its mid-point. A child weighing 160 N sits at one end. Calculate where another child of weight 200 N must sit to balance the seesaw. **(3 marks)**

Draw a diagram to help you.

Levers and gears

Levers and **gears** can transmit the **rotational effect** of forces.

Levers

A **lever** can be used to cause rotation. The nature of this rotation depends on the position of:

1 the **input force** – the force provided by the user of the lever

2 the **output force** – the force that results from the input force

3 the **fulcrum** – the turning point about which both forces act.

For different levers, the input force, output force and fulcrum are in different positions relative to each other.

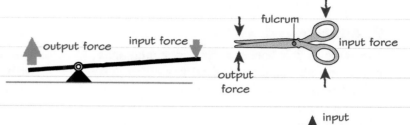

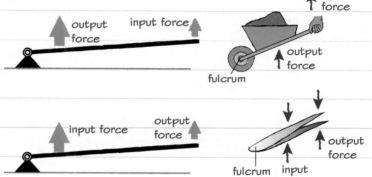

Gears

Gears are toothed wheels that are meshed together to transmit rotational force and motion. This is a low gear.

Each gear in a series reverses the direction of motion.

input

output

A larger gear will rotate more slowly than a smaller gear, but will have a greater turning effect. A low gear leads to a low speed and a high turning effect.

High gears and low gears

A high gear is when a large input gear turns a smaller output gear. This leads to a **high speed** and a **low turning effect**.

A low gear is when a smaller input gear turns a larger output gear. This leads to a **low speed** and a **high turning effect**.

Worked example

Describe the common features of gears and levers in terms of how they work.
(2 marks)

Gears and levers both transmit the rotational effect of a force and they can alter the size of the output force compared with the input force.

> You need to know that both gears and levers can cause rotation and can alter the size of the output force.

Now try this

Look at page 58 on moments. Consider the turning moment and describe how this affects the relative sizes of the forces.

1 Explain why a bicycle or a car needs different gears. **(3 marks)**

2 Explain why a heavy rock is easier to lift with a lever than without. **(4 marks)**

3 Explain how levers and gears transmit rotational forces. **(4 marks)**

Pressure

Pressure is a force acting per unit area. Fluids (liquids and gases) exert pressure which acts at right angles to a surface.

Pressure

Pressure is the force acting per unit area, measured at right angles to the area. Pressure is measured in pascals (Pa):
$1 \text{ Pa} = 1 \text{ N/m}^2$

You can use this equation to calculate pressure:

$$\frac{\text{pressure}}{\text{in Pa}} = \frac{\text{force normal to surface in N}}{\text{area of surface in m}^2}$$

$$p = \frac{F}{A}$$ **LEARN IT!** IT'S NOT ON THE EQUATIONS LIST

Atmospheric pressure

The atmosphere is a thin layer (compared with the size of the Earth) of air that surrounds the Earth.

The atmosphere can be thought of as a very high column of air above our bodies. This means that it will exert a pressure due to its weight, which acts normal to an area, A. Atmospheric pressure is about 100 000 Pa.

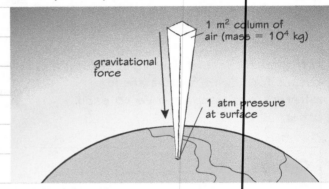

1 m² column of air (mass = 10^4 kg)

gravitational force

1 atm pressure at surface

The further up you go in the Earth's atmosphere, the less air there will be above you in the column of air – this means that there is less weight of air above you, and hence less pressure, the higher up you go.

Also the higher up you go in the atmosphere, the less dense the air becomes.

Worked example

(a) A force of 100 N acts normal to a block of wood of area 0.1 m² in contact with the floor. Calculate the pressure exerted. **(3 marks)**

$P = F \div A$
$= 100 \text{ N} \div 0.1 \text{ m}^2 = 1000 \text{ Pa}$

(b) The wooden block is turned on its end. The area in contact with the floor is now 0.01 m². Calculate the pressure exerted now. **(3 marks)**

$P = F \div A$
$= 100 \text{ N} \div 0.01 \text{ m}^2 = 10 000 \text{ Pa}$

(c) Explain why the pressure has increased. **(3 marks)**

same force, smaller area, so pressure is greater

A high force over a small area can produce a high pressure. A low force over a large area can produce a low pressure.

Now try this

Refer to density and upthrust in your answer.

1 The area of the sole of a trainer in contact with the floor is 0.025 m². A man with weight of 750 N is standing on one foot. Calculate the pressure exerted by the sole of the trainer on the floor. **(3 marks)**

2 Calculate the area over which a force of 600 N exerts a pressure of 20 kPa. **(4 marks)**

3 Explain why atmospheric pressure varies with height above a surface. **(3 marks)**

Distance and displacement

Distance and displacement are both measures of how far an object has moved, but they are not the same.

Distance

Distance is how far an object moves. It has only a magnitude, it does not involve a direction. Distance is a scalar quantity.

Examples of distances include 20 mm, 150 cm, 10 m and 500 km.

Displacement

Displacement involves both the distance that an object moves in a straight line and the direction in which it has moved from its starting point. Displacement is a vector quantity.

Examples of displacement include 20 mm to the left, 10 m North or 500 km on a bearing of 90°.

Describing distance

A man walks around a rectangular route, starting at point **A**, then visiting points **B**, **C** and **D**, before returning to **A**.

The total distance he has covered is 16 km. This is a measure of how far he has travelled in total.

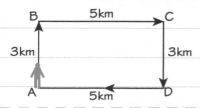

Describing displacement

A man walks around the same rectangular route, starting at point **A** and finishing at point **A**. The total distance he has covered is 16 km. However, his displacement at the end of the journey is 0 km, because he has returned to his starting point.

Displacement has a magnitude and a direction.

At **D** his displacement is 5 km East of **A**.

Worked example

A baby crawls 3 m from her cot at point **A** before turning through 90° at point **B** and crawling another 4 m, until she arrives at point **C**.

(a) Draw a diagram to show a possible route.

(3 marks)

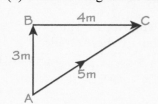

(b) Calculate the total distance crawled by the baby. **(2 marks)**

total distance = 3 m + 4 m = 7 m

(c) Calculate the size of the displacement from point **A**. **(2 marks)**

By scale drawing or use of Pythagoras' theorem, her displacement is 5 m from **A**.

Worked example

A runner takes part in a race that involves running along a path from a starting point, **A**, through a forest to the finish point, **B**. Draw a diagram that could show the possible distance covered and displacement of the runner at the end of the race. **(3 marks)**

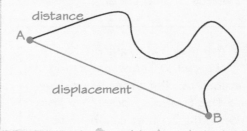

You can also find the direction of the baby's displacement from the scale drawing or by using trigonometry – it will be on a bearing of 53° from North.

Now try this

 1 Describe how the displacement of a pendulum changes as it swings. **(3 marks)**

 2 Explain how the displacement of an athlete at the end of a long race can be (a) zero **(2 marks)**; (b) positive **(2 marks)**; (c) negative. **(3 marks)**

Speed and velocity

Speed and velocity both measure how fast an object is moving but they are not the same.

Speed and velocity

Speed is **distance moved per unit time**. It can have units such as metres per second (m/s), kilometres per hour (km/h) or miles per hour (mph). Speed does not involve a direction and it is a **scalar quantity**.

The speed of a moving object is rarely the same value throughout the whole journey. The speed of sound and the speed of the wind also vary.

The velocity of an object is its **speed in a given direction**. Velocity is a **vector quantity**. A car that travels 500 m North in 20 seconds has a speed of 25 m/s but a velocity of 25 m/s North.

Typical everyday speeds

Example	Speed in m/s
walking	1.5
running	3
cycling	6
cars on UK roads	2 to 31
trains	up to 83 in the UK
sound waves in air	330
light waves	3×10^8

Calculating distance

For an object moving at a constant speed, the distance travelled in a certain amount of time is calculated using the equation:

$$\text{distance travelled in m} = \text{speed in m/s} \times \text{time in s}$$

$$s = v\,t$$

LEARN IT!
IT'S NOT ON THE EQUATIONS LIST

When the speed of the object changes over the course of a journey, it is better to use the equation:

$$\text{distance travelled in m} = \text{average speed in m/s} \times \text{time in s}$$

Average speed is the total distance travelled divided by the total time taken.

Maths skills You may be required to rearrange the equation in order to calculate distance, speed or time. Using the triangle, cover up the quantity you want to find out how to calculate it.

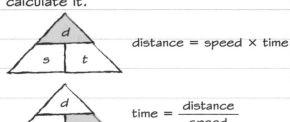

distance = speed × time

$$time = \frac{distance}{speed}$$

$$speed = \frac{distance}{time}$$

Changing velocity

A body can have a constant speed, but its velocity is constantly changing. This is because the distance being covered each second is constant, but the direction of motion is constantly changing.

Now try this

1 Give an example to show how speed is different from average speed.   **(4 marks)**
2 A car travels at a constant speed of 12 m/s for 60 s. How far has it travelled in this time?
                                                     (3 marks)
3 Explain how a body can be accelerating even when it is moving at a constant speed.   **(1 mark)**
4 Calculate the length of time it would take a runner to run 800 m at an average speed of 8 m/s.
                                                     (3 marks)

Distance–time graphs

The speed of an object can be calculated from the gradient of a distance–time graph.

Distance–time graphs

When an object moves in a straight line, you can represent the distance travelled on a distance–time graph. Distance–time graphs have distance on the *y*-axis and time on the *x*-axis. The shape of the graph tells us about the motion of the vehicle.

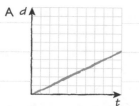
Constant or steady speed

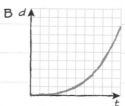
Accelerating (speeding up)

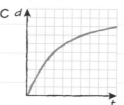
Decelerating (slowing down)

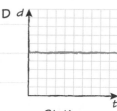
Stationary

Journeys

This distance–time graph tells you about a student's journey.

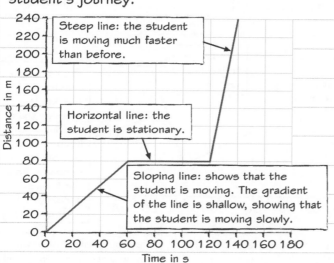

Steep line: the student is moving much faster than before.

Horizontal line: the student is stationary.

Sloping line: shows that the student is moving. The gradient of the line is shallow, showing that the student is moving slowly.

Speed

This distance–time graph shows another student's journey. You can work out the speed from the gradient of the distance–time graph.

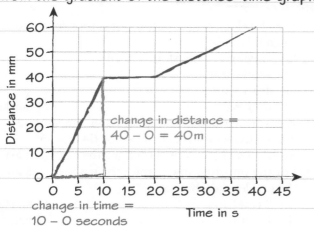

change in distance = 40 – 0 = 40 m

change in time = 10 – 0 seconds

Speed between 0 and 10 seconds =

$$\frac{\text{change in distance}}{\text{change in time}} = \frac{40\,\text{m}}{10\,\text{s}} = 4\,\text{m/s}$$

Now try this

1 Josh walks to school. He walks 400 m from his home in 250 seconds. He then meets his friend Asif and stops for 150 seconds. Both of them carry on to school walking 300 m in 300 seconds.
 (a) Draw a distance–time graph to represent the journey. **(4 marks)**
 (b) Work out Josh's average speed over the whole journey. **(3 marks)**
2 Look at the graph on the left.
 (a) What is happening between 10 and 20 seconds? **(1 mark)**
 (b) Work out the speed between 20 and 40 seconds. **(3 marks)**

Velocity–time graphs

Velocity–time graphs show how the velocity of a vehicle changes with time. You can also work out acceleration and distance travelled from the graph.

Interpreting velocity–time graphs

Velocity–time graphs have velocity plotted on the y-axis and time plotted on the x-axis. The graph shows you how the velocity changes with time.

The **slope** or **gradient** of the graph tells us the acceleration of the vehicle.

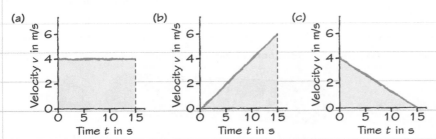

Maths skills Acceleration (gradient) = change in velocity/change in time.

(a) Acceleration = change in velocity ÷ change in time
$$= (4 - 4) \text{ m/s} \div (15 - 0) \text{ s}$$
$$= 0 \div 15 = 0 \text{ m/s}^2$$

(b) Acceleration $= (6 - 0)$ m/s $\div (15 - 0)$ s $= 6 \div 15$
$$= 0.4 \text{ m/s}^2$$

(c) Acceleration $= (0 - 4)$ m/s $\div (15 - 0)$ s $= -4 \div 15$
$$= -0.27 \text{ m/s}^2$$

Velocity–time graphs

This velocity–time graph shows how the velocity of a train along a straight track changes with time. You can work out the distance travelled by working out the area under the graph. You can also do this by counting the squares under the graph.

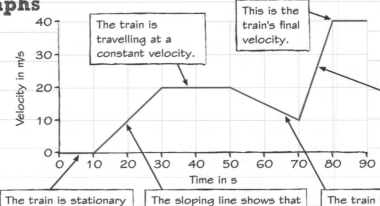

The train is travelling at a constant velocity.

This is the train's final velocity.

The train is accelerating. The line is steeper than the line between 10 and 30 seconds, so the train's acceleration is greater.

The train is stationary (its velocity is 0).

The sloping line shows that the train is accelerating.

The train is slowing down (its velocity is getting less).

Worked example

Use the velocity–time graph of the train to calculate the acceleration of the train between 50 s and 70 s.

(3 marks)

change in velocity = 10 m/s – 20 m/s
$$= -10 \text{ m/s}$$

change in time = 70 s – 50 s
$$= 20 \text{ s}$$

acceleration $= \dfrac{-10 \text{ m/s}}{20 \text{ s}}$
$$= -0.5 \text{ m/s}^2$$

Now try this

1 Sketch velocity–time graphs for a vehicle to show when it is:
   (a) moving at a constant velocity
   (b) accelerating
   (c) decelerating
   (d) stationary. **(4 marks)**

2 A car travels at a constant speed of 8 m/s for 12 s before accelerating at 1.5 m/s² for the next 6 s. Sketch a velocity–time graph for the car. **(4 marks)**

3 For the velocity–time graph shown above, calculate the acceleration between:
   (a) 0 s and 10 s **(2 marks)**
   (b) 10 s and 20 s **(2 marks)**
   (c) 30 s and 50 s **(2 marks)**
   (d) 50 s and 70 s. **(2 marks)**

Equations of motion

You can use equations to work out the velocity and acceleration of moving bodies.

Acceleration

Acceleration is a change in velocity per second. Acceleration is a vector quantity.

$$\text{acceleration in m/s}^2 = \frac{\text{change in velocity in m/s}}{\text{time taken in s}}$$

$$a = \frac{\Delta v}{t}$$

LEARN IT!
ITS NOT ON THE EQUATIONS LIST

Velocity

Velocity is the change in distance per second.

Velocity is a vector quantity.

(final velocity)² − (initial velocity)² = 2 × acceleration × distance

$$v^2 - u^2 = 2as$$

You can also write this as:

$$v^2 = u^2 + 2as$$

Worked example

A cat changes its speed from 2.5 m/s to 10.0 m/s over a period of 3.0 s. Calculate the cat's acceleration. **(3 marks)**

$v = 10\,\text{m/s}, u = 2.5\,\text{m/s}, t = 3\,\text{s}, a = ?$

$a = (\Delta v) \div t$

$\quad = (10.0\,\text{m/s} - 2.5\,\text{m/s}) \div 3.0\,\text{s}$

$\quad = 7.5\,\text{m/s} \div 3.0\,\text{s}$

$\quad = 2.5\,\text{m/s}^2$

Typical acceleration values

Object	Δv in m/s	t in s	a in m/s²
athlete	8.5	1.0	8.5
car	30	7.5	4
elevator	2	4	0.5
rollercoaster	200	10	20

The acceleration of a falling object is 9.8 m/s².

Watch out! When using this equation, the value for (Δv) may be negative, which means that the cat is slowing down.

Worked example

A motorcyclist passes through green traffic lights with an initial velocity of 4 m/s and then accelerates at a rate of 2.4 m/s², covering a total distance of 200 m. Calculate the final velocity of the motorcycle. **(4 marks)**

$u = 4\,\text{m/s}, a = 2.4\,\text{m/s}^2, x = 200\,\text{m}, v = ?$

$v^2 = u^2 + 2ax$

$\quad = (4)^2 + 2 \times 2.4 \times 200$

$\quad = 16 + 960 = 976$

$v = \sqrt{976} = 31.2\,\text{m/s}$

 Maths skills When working out s using this equation, you will need to rearrange it. Subtract u^2 from both sides and then divide both sides by 2a, to give $x = \dfrac{v^2 - u^2}{2a}$ substitute the other values and work out the value of s.

Watch out! When you substitute the values for u, a and s, you get a value for v^2. So you need to find the square root of this value to get the value for the final velocity, v.

Now try this

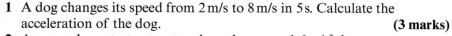

1 A dog changes its speed from 2 m/s to 8 m/s in 5 s. Calculate the acceleration of the dog. **(3 marks)**

2 An aeroplane starts at rest and accelerates at 1.6 m/s² down a runway. After 1800 m it takes off. Calculate its speed at take-off. **(3 marks)**

3 A car is travelling at 20 m/s. The traffic lights turn red 100 m ahead and the driver brakes. The acceleration of the car is −2 m/s². Will the car stop before it gets to the traffic lights? **(3 marks)**

If a vehicle is said to be 'starting from rest' then its initial velocity, u, will be zero, so the equation simplifies to $v^2 = 2as$.

Use the values to work out the final velocity of the car.

Terminal velocity

An object falling near to the Earth's surface will accelerate at first and may reach terminal velocity if it falls for long enough.

Free fall and terminal velocity

An object falling under the influence of gravity is said to be in free fall. An object that falls near to the Earth's surface will accelerate, initially, at a rate of $9.8 \, m/s^2$.

 An object starts to fall through a fluid such as water. The weight of the object makes it accelerate. Weight always acts downwards. The resistance of the fluid causes an upward force.

 As the falling object accelerates the resistance forces increase.

 When the resultant force is zero the object falls at a constant velocity called **terminal velocity**.

Terminal velocity and velocity–time graphs

Velocity–time graphs show the changing forces on a falling object.

The graph shows the stages in the fall of a skydiver.

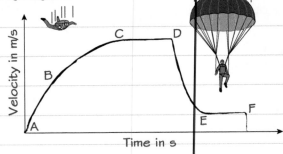

1 AB: The force of gravity pulls the skydiver downwards. Air resistance is small so the resultant force is large. The skydiver accelerates.

2 BC: As the velocity of the skydiver increases the air resistance increases. Weight remains constant. The resultant force gets smaller and the acceleration decreases.

3 CD: The air resistance is equal and opposite to the weight of the skydiver. The resultant force is zero so acceleration is zero. The skydiver has reached terminal velocity.

4 DE: The skydiver opens the parachute. The larger surface area increases the air resistance so that it is bigger than the weight. The resultant force is upwards. This means the acceleration downwards is negative. The skydiver's velocity reduces. As the velocity reduces, the air resistance decreases until it is again equal to the weight.

5 EF: The skydiver falls to the ground at a new lower terminal velocity and hits the ground at F and stops.

Worked example

A spherical ball is dropped into a long tube of viscous (thick) liquid. Sketch and label a velocity–time graph to show how the velocity of the ball changes throughout its descent. **(4 marks)**

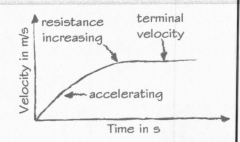

Now try this

1 Use the velocity–time graph at the top of this page to sketch a graph of the resultant force on the skydiver against time for the whole fall.
(4 marks)

2 Explain why the velocity–time graph for the ball in the worked example is different from the graph for the parachutist higher up the page.
(4 marks)

Newton's first law

A body will remain at rest or continue in a straight line at a constant speed as long as the forces acting on it are **balanced**.

Stationary bodies

The forces acting on a stationary body are balanced.

The forces acting on the object are balanced.

tension 25 N

weight 25 N

A common mistake is to think that when the resultant force on an object is zero, the object is stationary. The object may also be travelling at a constant speed.

Bodies moving at a constant speed

The forces acting on a body moving at a constant speed, and in a straight line, are balanced.

reaction force 15 kN

resistive force 20 kN

driving force 20 kN

weight 15 kN

The forces on the car are balanced. The car will continue to move at a constant speed in a straight line (constant velocity) until another external force is applied.

Unbalanced forces

5 N   10 N

This body will accelerate to the right, since there is a resultant force of 5 N acting to the right.

Worked example

Explain the effect that each of these forces will have on a car.

(a) 300 N driving force from the engine, 200 N resistive force. **(3 marks)**

resultant force = 300 N − 200 N = 100 N
The car will accelerate in the direction of the resultant force.
Its velocity will increase.

A resultant force acting in the opposite direction to the movement of a body will slow it down. It can also reverse the direction of motion.

(b) 200 N forward force from the engine, 400 N friction from brakes. **(3 marks)**

resultant force = 200 N − 400 N = −200 N (200 N acting backwards)

The car will accelerate in the direction of the resultant force. This is in the opposite direction to its velocity, so the car will slow down.

(c) 300 N forward force, 300 N drag. **(3 marks)**

resultant force = 0 N

The car will continue to move at the same velocity.

Now try this

1   State what forces act on a body that is moving at a constant speed. **(2 marks)**

2   Explain how the direction of a moving body can be made to change. **(2 marks)**

3   Draw diagrams to show how two forces of 100 N acting on a mass can make it:
    (a) stationary **(2 marks)**
    (b) move at a constant speed **(2 marks)**
    (c) accelerate to the left. **(2 marks)**

Newton's second law

When a resultant force acts on a mass then there will be a change in its velocity. The resultant force determines the size and direction of the subsequent acceleration of the mass.

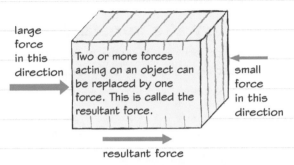

large force in this direction

Two or more forces acting on an object can be replaced by one force. This is called the resultant force.

small force in this direction

resultant force

Forces have direction, so a force of −1 N is in the opposite direction to a force of 1 N.

When two or more forces act on the same straight line or are parallel, they can be added together to find the **resultant force**.

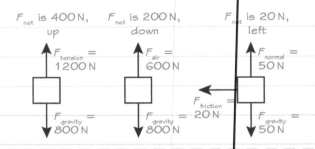

F_{net} is 400 N, up

$F_{tension} = 1200\,N$

$F_{gravity} = 800\,N$

F_{net} is 200 N, down

$F_{air} = 600\,N$

$F_{gravity} = 800\,N$

F_{net} is 20 N, left

$F_{normal} = 50\,N$

$F_{friction} = 20\,N$

$F_{gravity} = 50\,N$

Force, mass and acceleration

The acceleration of an object is proportional to the resultant force acting on the object and inversely proportional to the mass of the object. The equation connecting force, mass and acceleration is:

$$\frac{\text{resultant force}}{\text{in N}} = \frac{\text{mass}}{\text{in kg}} \times \frac{\text{acceleration}}{\text{in m/s}^2}$$

$F = m\,a$

LEARN IT!
IT'S NOT ON THE EQUATIONS LIST

- The acceleration is in the same direction as the force.
- When the resultant force is zero, the acceleration is zero.
- A negative force means that the object is accelerating backwards or is slowing down.

Worked example

The diagram shows the horizontal forces acting on a boat. The boat has a mass of 400 kg.

resistive force 600 N

driving force 900 N

Calculate the acceleration of the boat at the instant shown in the diagram. **(3 marks)**

resultant force on boat = 900 N – 600 N = 300 N forwards

mass = 400 kg

acceleration $= \frac{F}{m} = \frac{300\,N}{400\,kg}$

$\frac{F}{m \times a}$

$= 0.75\,m/s^2$

Worked example

A basketball player catches a ball. The force acting on the ball is −1.44 N and its acceleration is −2.4 m/s².

(a) Which of the following describes the effect of the force on the ball? **(1 mark)**

☐ The ball is moving backwards.
☒ The ball is slowing down moving forwards.
☐ The ball is moving faster forwards.
☐ The ball is slowing down moving backwards.

(b) Calculate the mass of the ball. **(3 marks)**

$m = \frac{F}{a}$

$= \frac{-1.4\,N}{-2.4\,m/s^2} = 0.583\,kg \sim 0.6\,kg$

The symbol ~ indicates an approximate value or approximate answer.

Now try this

1 Calculate the resultant force that causes a 1.2 kg mass to accelerate at 8 m/s². **(3 marks)**

2 Calculate the size of the mass that accelerates at 0.8 m/s² when the resultant force is 18.8 N. **(3 marks)**

3 Calculate the acceleration of a mass of 80 g when the resultant force is 0.6 kN. **(5 marks)**

Force, mass and acceleration

Practical skills You can determine the relationship of force, mass and acceleration by varying the force on an object of constant mass, and measuring the time that it takes to pass between two light gates that are a small distance apart.

Required practical

Investigating force and acceleration

Aim

to investigate the effect of force on acceleration of a glider

Apparatus

linear air track and gliders, bench pulley, string, weight stack and weights, card of known length, clamp stands, clamps and bosses, light gates

Method

1 Set up the apparatus as shown.

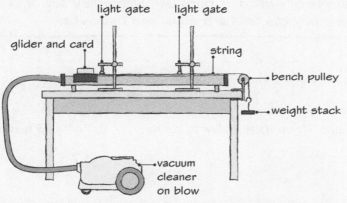

light gate   light gate

glider and card

string

bench pulley

weight stack

vacuum cleaner on blow

2 Set up the light gates to take the velocity and time readings for you.

3 Switch on the vacuum cleaner to start the glider moving.

4 Record velocity and time for different values of weight on the weight stack.

5 Work out acceleration by dividing the difference in the velocity values by the time taken for the card to pass between both gates.

Results

You can record your results in a table like this.

Force in N	Acceleration in cm/s²			
	First reading	Second reading	Third reading (if necessary)	Mean

Plot a graph of acceleration against force.

Conclusion

The acceleration of the glider is proportional to the force acting on the glider.

There is more information about the relationship between force, mass and acceleration on page 68.

An accelerating mass of greater than a few hundred grams can be dangerous, and may hurt somebody if it hits them at speed. Bear this in mind when designing your investigation.

It is better to use light gates and other electronic equipment to record values as this is more accurate than using a ruler and a stopwatch.

Maths skills   Velocity and acceleration

Key points to remember for this investigation are:

Acceleration is change in speed ÷ time taken, so two velocity values are needed, along with the time difference between these readings, to obtain a value for the acceleration of the trolley.

Velocity is the rate of change of displacement and acceleration is the rate of change of velocity. The word rate means 'per unit time':

$$v = \frac{\Delta x}{\Delta t} \quad \text{and} \quad a = \frac{\Delta v}{\Delta t}$$

Now try this

1 Explain why it is better to use light gates and a data logger than a stopwatch to record time values. **(3 marks)**

2 Suggest how the investigation described above could be improved to obtain better results. **(4 marks)**

3 Design a similar experiment to determine how acceleration depends on the mass of the glider. **(5 marks)**

Newton's third law

Whenever two objects interact, the forces that they exert on each other are equal and opposite.

Action and reaction

Newton's third law states that for every action there is an equal and opposite reaction.

The action force and the reaction force **act on different bodies**.

100 N from the man

100 N from the wall

The man and wall are in equilibrium because the forces in the system are all balanced. There is no overall force in any direction. The two forces are an example of an **action–reaction pair**.

Newton's third law examples

Watch out! Just because two forces are equal and opposite it does not always mean that they are an example of Newton's third law.

The reaction force of the table pushing up on the book, and the force of gravity acting downwards, are both

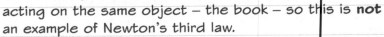

$R = -F = -mg$

$F = mg$

acting on the same object – the book – so this is **not** an example of Newton's third law.

The gravitational pull of the Earth on the book and the gravitational pull of the book on the Earth **are** an example of Newton's third law, since they act on different objects, and are equal and opposite.

Worked example

Identify five equal and opposite forces below that show Newton's third law in action.   **(5 marks)**

1 The elephant's feet push backward on the ground; the ground pushes forward on its feet.

2 The right end of the right rope pulls leftward on the elephant's body; its body pulls rightward on the right end of the right rope.

3 The left end of the right rope pulls rightward on the man; the man pulls leftward on the left end of the right rope.

4 The right end of the left rope pulls leftward on the man; the man pulls rightward on the right end of the left rope.

5 The tractor pulls leftward on the left end of the left rope; the left end of the left rope pulls rightward on the tractor.

Now try this

1 State Newton's third law. **(3 marks)**

2 A goalkeeper catches a football from a penalty kick. Explain how Newton's third law applies to the goalkeeper's gloves in this situation. **(3 marks)**

Stopping distance

Stopping distance is the **total distance** over which a vehicle comes to rest.

It takes time for a moving car to come to a stop, and the car is still moving during this time. Understanding the factors that affect stopping distance is important for road safety.

Danger appears.   Driver brakes.   Car has stopped.

thinking distance = the distance the car travels while the driver reacts to the danger and applies the brakes

braking distance = the distance the car travels while it is slowing down, once the brakes have been applied

stopping distance = thinking distance + braking distance

Factors affecting stopping distance

Thinking distance and braking distance increase when the car's speed increases.

When you double the speed of a car, the thinking distance doubles, but the braking distance increases by a factor of four.

Thinking distance (driver's reaction time) increases when:
- the driver is **tired**
- the driver is **distracted**
- the driver has taken **alcohol** or **drugs**.

Braking distance increases when:
- the amount of **friction** between the tyre and the road decreases
- the road is **icy** or **wet**
- the brakes or tyres are **worn**
- the **mass** of the car is bigger.

Thinking distance and braking distance

Thinking distance is directly proportional to speed. If the thinking distance is 6 m when the car is travelling at 20 mph, then it will be 12 m when the car is travelling at 40 mph.

Braking distance is proportional to (speed)².

20 mph   6 m 6 m   = 12 m (40 ft) or 3

40 mph   12 m   24 m   = 36 m (120 ft) or 9

To bring a vehicle to rest, work must be done on it. When a force, F, is applied to the brakes, the kinetic energy, $\frac{1}{2}mv^2$, is transferred to thermal energy and the vehicle comes to rest over a certain distance, s. Large decelerations may lead to brakes overheating and/or loss of control.

The equation that governs this is:

$$Fs = \frac{1}{2}mv^2$$

Worked example

A car is moving at a constant speed. Explain how the stopping distance changes when:
(a) the speed of the car increases **(2 marks)**
(b) the car has more passengers **(2 marks)**
(c) the driver has been drinking alcohol. **(2 marks)**

(a) The stopping distance increases because the thinking distance and braking distance increase.

(b) The mass of the car will be greater so the braking distance will increase, which means that the stopping distance will increase.

(c) The stopping distance will increase because the thinking distance will increase.

Now try this

1 Explain how the thinking and braking distance of a car changes when the speed of the car increases from 20 mph to 80 mph. **(2 marks)**

2 A car of mass 1250 kg is travelling at 12 m/s. Calculate:

Use the equation $Fs = \frac{1}{2}mv^2$

(a) the kinetic energy of the car when it is moving at this speed **(3 marks)**
(b) the braking distance of the car if the average force applied to the brakes is 1800 N. **(3 marks)**

Reaction time

Human reaction time is the time between a **stimulus** occurring and a **response**. It is related to how quickly the human brain can process information and react to it.

Human reaction time

It takes a typical person between 0.2 s and 0.9 s to react to a stimulus. Some people, such as international cricketers, 100-m sprinters and fighter pilots, train themselves to have improved reaction times.

Reaction times and driving

Drivers have to react to changes in the traffic when driving. This may involve reacting to traffic lights changing colour, traffic slowing on a motorway, or avoiding people or animals.

The reaction time of humans may be affected by:

- ☑ tiredness
- ☑ distractions.
- ☑ alcohol and drugs

Measuring reaction time

You can determine human reaction time by using the ruler drop test.

The reaction time is determined from the equation:

$$\text{reaction time} = \sqrt{\frac{2 \times \text{distance ruler falls}}{\text{gravitational field strength}}}$$

Repeats can be used to get a mean value for the reaction time.

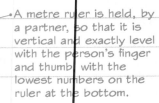

• A metre ruler is held, by a partner, so that it is vertical and exactly level with the person's finger and thumb with the lowest numbers on the ruler at the bottom.

A person sits with their index finger and thumb opened to a gap of about 5 cm.

• The ruler is dropped and then grasped by the other person. The distance fallen is given by where the person has caught the ruler.

Worked example

A ruler drop test is conducted five times with the same person. The results show that the five distances fallen are: 0.16 m, 0.17 m, 0.18 m, 0.16 m and 0.15 m.

(a) Calculate the mean distance that the ruler drops. **(3 marks)**

$$\text{mean} = \frac{(0.16 + 0.17 + 0.18 + 0.16 + 0.15)}{5}$$

$$= 0.16\,\text{m}$$

(b) Calculate the person's reaction time. **(3 marks)**

$$\text{reaction time} = \sqrt{\frac{2 \times 0.16}{10}} = 0.18\,\text{s}$$

Worked example

(a) A driver in a car moving at 30 km/h has a reaction time of 0.25 s. Calculate the distance the car travels between seeing a hazard in the road and then applying the brakes. **(4 marks)**

distance (m) = speed (m/s) × time (s)

$$30\,\text{km/h} = \frac{30000\,\text{m}}{3600\,\text{s}} = 8.3\,\text{m/s}$$

distance travelled = 8.3 m/s × 0.25 s = 2.1 m

(b) Describe how distractions affect the thinking distance of a driver. **(2 marks)**

Distractions to a driver will increase the reaction time and this causes the thinking distance to increase.

Now try this

1 (a) Define human reaction time. **(1 mark)**
   (b) Give the typical range for reaction time. **(2 marks)**
   (c) Give **three** factors that can cause reaction time to increase. **(3 marks)**

2 Explain why the reaction time doubles when the distance that a ruler falls increases by a factor of 4. **(2 marks)**

3 Calculate the difference in distance that a ruler will fall for a person with a reaction time of 0.2 s compared with a person with a reaction time of 0.9 s. **(4 marks)**

Extended response – Forces

There will be at least one 6-mark question on your exam paper. For these questions, you will need to think scientifically and structure your answer logically, showing how the points you make are related to each other. You can revise the topics for this question, which is about forces, on pages 50–72.

Worked example

The diagram shows a trolley, ramp and light gates being used to investigate the relationship between the acceleration of a trolley on a slope and the angle that the slope makes with the horizontal.

Describe a simple investigation to determine how the acceleration of the trolley depends on the angle of the slope.

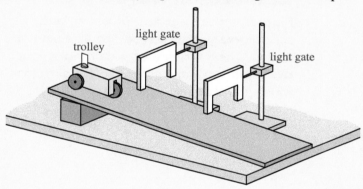

trolley   light gate   light gate

(6 marks)

I will start with the ramp at an angle of 10° and roll the trolley down the slope from the same starting position along the slope each time. The mass of the trolley needs to be kept constant, and a suitable value would be 500 g. I will then increase the ramp angle by 5° each time until I have at least 6 readings. I will repeat readings to check for accuracy and precision.

The speed of the trolley at each light gate is calculated using the equation speed = distance ÷ time, where the distance recorded is the length of the card that passes through the light gates. The acceleration of the trolley is calculated by finding the difference in the speed values at the two light gates and then dividing this by the time it takes the trolley to pass between the gates.

I would expect the acceleration of the trolley to increase as the angle increases, although the relationship may not be linear. This is because, as the slope angle increases, you increase the component of the trolley's weight that is acting down the slope, which is the force responsible for the trolley's acceleration.

Command word: Describe

When you are asked to **describe** something, you need to write down facts, events or processes accurately.

Your answer should refer to the equations needed to calculate the velocity and acceleration of the trolley, as well as how you will show the relationship between acceleration and angle of slope.

You need to be careful when stating what you will vary and what you will keep the same. Since the dependent variable is acceleration and the independent variable is angle of slope, you will need to keep the mass of the trolley and its starting point the same each time.

Be clear when referring to how the speed of the trolley will be measured by referring to the card that passes through the light gates, and mention that the length of the card needs to be known if the light gates are recording time values. You need two speed and time values to calculate the acceleration.

You can also refer to the increase in gravitational potential energy as the slope angle increases. This means more is transferred to kinetic energy and so a greater change in velocity per second.

Now try this

The distance taken for vehicles to stop on roads depends on a number of factors. Discuss what these factors are and how they affect stopping distance.

(6 marks)

Waves

Waves transfer energy and information without transferring matter. Evidence of this for a water wave can be seen when a ball dropped into a pond bobs up and down, but the wave energy travels outwards as ripples across the surface of the pond.

Waves can be described by their:
- **frequency** – the number of waves passing a point each second, measured in **hertz (Hz)**
- **speed** – measured in **metres per second (m/s)**
- **wavelength** and **amplitude**
- **period** – the time taken for one wavelength to pass a point
- **period** in s = $\dfrac{1}{\text{frequency in Hz}}$

$$T = \frac{1}{f}$$

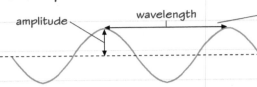

Wavelength is the distance between two equivalent adjacent points on a wave.

Watch out! Remember that the amplitude is *half* of the distance from the top to the bottom of the wave. Amplitude is the maximum displacement of a point on a wave from its undisturbed position. Students often get this wrong.

Longitudinal waves

Sound waves are **longitudinal** waves. The particles in the material through which the sound is travelling move back and forth along the same direction that the sound is travelling.

Particles in a **longitudinal** wave move **along** the same direction as the wave.

Transverse waves

Ripples on the surface of water, and **electromagnetic waves** are all **transverse** waves. The particles of water move in a direction at right angles to the direction in which the wave is travelling.

Particles in a transverse wave move across the direction in which the wave is travelling.

Remember, it is the wave that transfers energy and not the wave or air itself that travels.

Worked example

Give two ways in which longitudinal and transverse waves are

(a) similar   **(2 marks)**

They both transfer energy without transferring matter and have an amplitude, speed, wavelength and frequency.

(b) different.   **(2 marks)**

Particles in longitudinal waves vibrate along the direction of movement, whereas particles in transverse waves move at 90 degrees to the direction of travel. They can also have different speeds, frequencies and wavelengths.

Now try this

1 (a) Sketch a transverse wave and mark the amplitude and wavelength on it.   **(3 marks)**

   (b) Draw an arrow to show which way the wave moves.   **(1 mark)**

   (c) Draw a small particle on the wave, with arrows to show which way it moves.   **(1 mark)**

2 (a) Calculate the time period of a sound wave with a frequency of 400 Hz.   **(3 marks)**

   (b) Calculate the frequency of a water wave with a time period of 0.2 s.   **(3 marks)**

Wave equation

The wave equation relates the wave speed, frequency and wavelength of any wave.

Wave equation

All waves, whether longitudinal or transverse, obey the wave equation:

$$\frac{\text{wave speed}}{\text{in m/s}} = \frac{\text{frequency}}{\text{in Hz}} \times \frac{\text{wavelength}}{\text{in m}}$$

$$v = f\lambda$$

 **LEARN IT!** IT'S NOT ON THE EQUATIONS LIST

Typical values for waves

Some typical values for sound waves in air, water waves in a ripple tank, light waves in air and seismic S waves are shown.

Wave	v in m/s	f in Hz	λ in m
sound	340	3000	0.11
water	5	5	1.0
light	3×10^8	6×10^{14}	5×10^{-7}
S-wave	4000	40	100

Worked example

A seismic wave has a frequency of 15 Hz and travels at 4050 m/s. Calculate its wavelength. **(4 marks)**

$$\lambda = \frac{v}{f}$$
$$= \frac{4050 \,\text{m/s}}{15 \,\text{Hz}}$$
$$= 270 \,\text{m}$$

λ is the Greek letter 'lambda'.

Maths skills Start with the equation $v = f\lambda$ and rearrange it to make λ the subject.

Divide both sides of the equation by f, to get

$$\lambda = \frac{v}{f}$$

Substitute the values for v and f to calculate the value for the wavelength, λ.

The units for v are m/s and the units for f are Hz (or per second), so the units for λ are $\frac{\text{m/s}}{1/s} = $ m.

Always state the correct units as part of your answer.

Worked example

A ripple on the surface of water in a ripple tank has a frequency of 4 Hz and a wavelength of 5 cm. Calculate the wave speed of the ripples.

(3 marks)

wave speed = frequency × wavelength
= 4 Hz × 0.05 m = 0.2 m/s

Convert wavelength to metres.

Worked example

An X-ray has a wavelength of 1×10^{-10} m. Calculate the frequency of an X-ray in air.

(3 marks)

wave speed = frequency × wavelength
so frequency = wave speed ÷ wavelength

$$= \frac{3 \times 10^8 \,\text{m/s}}{1 \times 10^{-10} \,\text{m}} = 3 \times 10^{18} \,\text{Hz}$$

Rearrange the wave equation to make f the subject.

Now try this

 1 Calculate the wave speed of a sound wave with a frequency of 14 000 Hz and a wavelength of 0.024 m. **(3 marks)**

 2 Calculate the frequency of a radio wave in air with a wavelength of 1200 m. **(3 marks)**

3 Calculate the wavelength of a gamma-ray source of frequency 2×10^{20} Hz. **(3 marks)**

Measuring wave velocity

You need to be able to **calculate** the speed of sound in air or the speed of ripples on the surface of water.

Calculating the speed of sound in air

Method 1: using an echo.

1 Measure the distance from the source of the sound to the reflecting surface (the wall).

2 Measure the time interval, with a stopwatch, between the original sound being produced and the echo being heard.

3 Use $\dfrac{\text{speed}}{\text{in m/s}} = \dfrac{\text{distance}}{\text{in m}} \div \dfrac{\text{time}}{\text{in s}}$ to calculate the speed of sound in air.

Repeat the experiment a number of times over a range of distances to obtain accurate and precise results.

Method 2: using two microphones and an oscilloscope.

1 Set up the microphones one in front of the other at different distances in a straight line from a loudspeaker.

2 Set the frequency of the sound from the loudspeaker to a known, audible value.

3 Display the two waveforms on the oscilloscope. Measure the distance between the microphones.

4 Move the microphones apart so that the waveforms move apart by 1 wavelength.

5 Calculate the speed of sound using the equation:
$\dfrac{\text{wavespeed}}{\text{in m/s}} = \dfrac{\text{frequency}}{\text{in Hz}} \times \dfrac{\text{wavelength}}{\text{in m}}$

Calculating the speed of ripples on water surfaces

You can work out the speed of ripples on the surface of water using a ripple tank and a strobe.

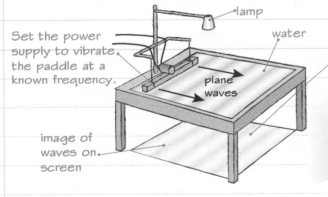

Set the power supply to vibrate the paddle at a known frequency.

lamp

water

plane waves

image of waves on screen

Use a strobe light to 'freeze' the water waves so that you can measure the wavelength.

strobe light

Use the equation
wave speed = frequency × wavelength
to calculate the speed or velocity of the water waves on the surface of the ripple tank.

Worked example

(a) A hand clap is made 480 m from a wall and the echo is heard 3 seconds later. Calculate the speed of sound. **(3 marks)**

speed = distance ÷ time = 960 m ÷ 3 s = 320 m/s

(b) Method 2 is used to determine the speed of sound. The distance between the two microphones is 35 cm and it represents one wavelength. The frequency of the sound is 1 kHz. Calculate the speed of sound in air. **(3 marks)**

wave speed = frequency × wavelength = 1000 Hz × 0.35 m = 350 m/s

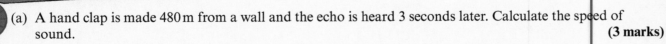

Now try this

1 The frequency of a ripple tank paddle is 4 Hz and the wavelength of the ripples is 8 cm. Calculate the speed of the water waves in m/s. **(3 marks)**

2 Describe how you could obtain an accurate value for the speed of sound in air. **(4 marks)**

Waves in fluids

🧪 **Practical skills**   You can **determine the wave speed, frequency and wavelength** of waves by using appropriate apparatus.

Required practical

See pages 74–76 for the properties of waves, including the relationship between wave speed, frequency and wavelength.

Investigating waves

Aim

to investigate the suitability of apparatus to measure the speed, frequency and wavelength of waves in a fluid

Apparatus

ripple tank, motor, plane wave generator, stroboscope, ruler, A3 paper and pencil

Water and electricity are being used here, both of which can be dangerous. Be careful to take this into consideration when planning your practical.

Method

1 Set up the apparatus as shown.

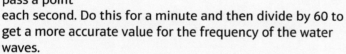

2 Calculate the frequency of the waves by counting the number of waves that pass a point each second. Do this for a minute and then divide by 60 to get a more accurate value for the frequency of the water waves.

3 Use a stroboscope to 'freeze' the waves and find their wavelength by using a ruler. The ruler can be left in the tank or the waves can be projected onto a piece of A3 paper under the tank and the wave positions marked with pencil marks on the paper.

4 Calculate the wave speed.

To obtain accurate results for the wavelength of the water wave, it is best to find the distance between a large number of waves and then divide this value by the number of waves. This will reduce the percentage error in your value when determining a value for the wavelength of the wave.

Waves in water

Water waves will travel at a constant speed in a ripple tank when generated at different frequencies if the depth of the water is constant at all points. This means that the equation wave speed = frequency × wavelength will give the same wave speed – if the frequency increases, then the wavelength will decrease in proportion.

Results

Wavelength in m	Frequency in Hz	Wave speed in m/s
0.05	10.0	5.0
0.10	5.0	5.0
0.15	3.0	4.5
0.20	2.5	5.0

Conclusion

A ripple tank can be used to determine values for the wavelength, frequency and wave speed of water waves. It is a suitable method, provided that small wavelengths and frequencies are used.

Now try this

1 Describe the main errors in determining the speed of water waves in this investigation. **(3 marks)**

2 Explain how the investigation described here can be improved. **(4 marks)**

Waves and boundaries

Waves can show different effects when they move from one material to another. These changes can occur at the **boundary** or **interface** between the two materials.

Waves and boundaries

Whenever a sound wave, light wave or water wave reaches the boundary between two materials, the wave can be:

- **reflected**
- **refracted**
- **transmitted** or
- **absorbed**.

Waves are transmitted if they pass through a body, for example when radio waves pass through walls and are detected by a radio receiver.

Waves are absorbed when they are taken in by a body and do not pass through it, for example when microwaves are absorbed by food in a microwave oven.

Reflection at a surface

Light waves, water waves and sound waves can all be reflected at a surface, which acts as the boundary between two different materials.

angle i = angle r

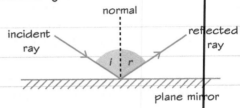

Refraction

Refraction is the change in the direction of a light ray that happens when it travels from one transparent material into another. Notice that the ray of light bends *towards* the normal as it enters the glass and *away* from the normal when it leaves the glass.

Rays of light that meet a surface at 90° do not bend at all but simply continue into the material without a change in direction.

Worked example

Explain why an infrared remote control will sometimes operate a TV in the same room when pointed at a wall, but it will not operate a TV on the other side of the wall. **(3 marks)**

Some of the infrared waves reach the TV because they are reflected by the wall and change direction. They do not reach the TV on the other side of the wall because they are absorbed/not transmitted by the wall.

Refraction special case

When light, sound or water waves move from one material into another, their **direction does not change** if they are moving along the normal.

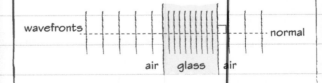

Now try this

1 State **four** things that can happen to a wave at a boundary between two materials. **(2 marks)**

2 Explain why you can get sunburnt when you are outside on a sunny day, but not when you are in a room that has no windows. **(3 marks)**

3 Suggest how the absorption of different wavelengths of infrared radiation by molecules in the atmosphere is:
(a) useful **(2 marks)**
(b) a problem. **(2 marks)**

Investigating refraction

Practical skills You can investigate the refraction of light by different substances and reflection of light by different types of surface.

Required practical

Aim

to investigate how light waves change direction when they move from air into other transparent materials

Apparatus

ray box lens and slits, 12-V power supply, glass block, Perspex block, ruler, protractor, A3 paper, sharp pencil

Method

1 Place the rectangular block on the A3 paper and draw around it with the sharp pencil.

2 Draw the normal line, which will be at right angles to the side of the block towards which the light ray will be shone.

glass block

r

i

normal

ray box

3 Using the protractor and pencil, mark on the paper angles of incidence of 0° through to 80° in 10° intervals.

4 Starting with the 0° angle (the light ray travelling along the normal line), direct the light ray towards the block and mark its exit point from the block with a sharp pencil dot.

5 Remove the glass block and join the dot to the point of incidence by drawing a straight line. Measure and record this angle, which is the angle of refraction.

6 Repeat for all of the other angles from 10° to 80°.

7 Repeat for the Perspex block.

Results

Angle of incidence in °	Angle of refraction in °	
	Glass	Perspex
0	0	0
10	7	7
20	13	13
30	19	20
40	25	27
50	31	33
60	35	40

Conclusion

When a light ray travels from air into a glass block, its direction changes and the angle of refraction will be less than the angle of incidence unless it is travelling along the normal.

The angle of refraction for the same angle of incidence should be smaller in glass than in Perspex because the glass is more optically dense and slows the light down more.

There is more information about the refraction of light on page 78.

When carrying out the investigation, make sure that you direct a thin beam of light towards the point at which the normal makes contact with the glass block. Clearly mark the angles from 0° to 80° with a sharp pencil and ruler.

Be careful! The ray box is likely to get hot when in use for long periods of time, so be careful not to burn your skin.

Remember that the angle of incidence is measured with respect to the normal line.

Light will slow down more when it travels from air into glass than it will when it travels from air into water. This is because the 'optical density' of glass is greater than that of air.

Refraction

The refraction of a light ray involves a change in:

☑ the direction of the light ray

☑ the speed of the light.

Light slows down when it moves from air into glass and speeds up when it moves from glass into air.

The only time when the direction does not change is when the beam is travelling along the normal.

Now try this

1 State the **two** things that can change when a light ray is refracted. **(2 marks)**

2 Explain what results you would expect if you repeated this investigation for a third material that was a rectangular block containing water. **(2 marks)**

3 Explain how the (a) frequency and (b) wavelength of a light ray are affected when it enters glass from air. **(4 marks)**

Electromagnetic spectrum

Electromagnetic waves form a continuous spectrum of waves that transfer energy from a source to an absorber. The waves are similar in many respects and different in others.

All electromagnetic waves...

- are **transverse waves** (the electromagnetic vibrations are at right angles to the direction the wave is travelling – see page 74)
- travel at the **same speed** (3×10^8 m/s) in a **vacuum**
- **transfer energy** to the observer.

Energy transfer examples

- Infrared, visible and ultraviolet radiation transfer energy from the Sun to the Earth.
- Radio waves transfer energy from TV and radio transmitters to TVs and radios.
- Microwave ovens transfer energy to food by microwaves, which are absorbed by water molecules in food.

The electromagnetic spectrum

As the **frequency** of the radiation **increases**, the **wavelength decreases**.

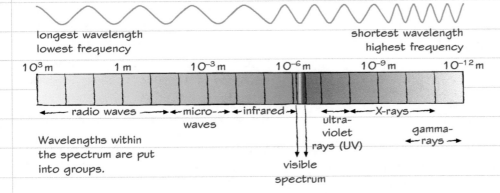

longest wavelength
lowest frequency

shortest wavelength
highest frequency

10^3 m   1 m 10^{-3} m 10^{-6} m 10^{-9} m 10^{-12} m

← radio waves → ← micro-waves → ← infrared → ← ultra-violet rays (UV) → ← X-rays → ← gamma-rays →

visible spectrum

Wavelengths within the spectrum are put into groups.

Our eyes detect visible light only from 4×10^{-7} m to 7×10^{-7} m which is the limited range of the electromagnetic spectrum. Red light is at the long wavelength end and violet is at the short wavelength end.

Worked example

(a) List the main groups of electromagnetic waves from longest to shortest wavelength. **(1 mark)**

radio, microwave, infrared, visible, ultraviolet, X-rays, gamma

(b) Calculate the frequency of an electromagnetic wave travelling in air that has a wavelength of 5×10^{-7} m. **(4 marks)**

frequency = wave speed ÷ wavelength

$$frequency = \frac{3 \times 10^8}{5 \times 10^{-7}}$$

$$= 6 \times 10^{14} \, Hz$$

Worked example

Describe examples of the transfer of energy by:
(a) radio waves   **(1 mark)**
(b) microwaves   **(1 mark)**
(c) infrared radiation.   **(1 mark)**

(a) TV signals sent from a transmitter to a receiver

(b) mobile phone signals being sent or microwaves being used to cook food

(c) radiation from a hot source being detected by the skin or TV remote control signals being used to change channel

Now try this

1 State the type of electromagnetic radiation that has:
   (a) the longest wavelength   **(1 mark)**
   (b) the highest frequency.   **(1 mark)**

2 The human eye detects wavelengths that range from 4×10^{-7} m to 7×10^{-7} m. Work out the range of frequencies that the eye detects.   **(3 marks)**

3 An electromagnetic source produces 4×10^{18} waves in 1 minute.
   (a) Calculate the wavelength of the source.   **(3 marks)**
   (b) State what part of the electromagnetic spectrum this radiation belongs to. **(1 mark)**

Infrared radiation

Practical skills You can investigate the relationship between the **rate** at which a material **emits** or **absorbs thermal radiation** and the nature of its **surface**.

Required practical

Aim

to investigate how the nature of a surface affects the rate at which it absorbs or radiates thermal energy

Apparatus

Leslie's cube, thermometers, stopwatch, ruler, clamp, boss and retort stand

Method 1: radiating thermal energy

1 Fill the Leslie's cube with hot water at a known temperature. Place a thermometer a small distance away from each of the sides. Plug the top of the cube with a bung.

2 Measure the temperature at a distance of 10 cm from each of the four sides of Leslie's cube for a period of 5 minutes, taking a reading every 30 seconds.

Method 2: absorbing thermal energy

1 Fill the Leslie's cube with the same volume of cold water at a known temperature. Plug the top of the cube with a thermometer and bung.

2 Heat each side, one at a time, with a radiant heater from the same distance away (about 10 cm).

3 Record how the temperature of the water changes, every 30 seconds, over an appropriate period of time.

Results

Method 1: plot graphs of temperature against time for each of the four surfaces on the same axes.

	Dull black	Shiny black	Silver	White
Start	80 °C	80 °C	80 °C	80 °C
Finish	56 °C	62 °C	74 °C	68 °C

Method 2: plot a graph of temperature against time.

	Dull black	Shiny black	Silver	White
Start	20 °C	20 °C	20 °C	20 °C
Finish	34 °C	28 °C	22 °C	24 °C

Conclusion

Typical results obtained are shown in the table.

	Dull black	Shiny black	White	Silver
Emitter	best	second	third	worst
Absorber	best	second	third	worst

There is more information on the emission and absorption of thermal energy on pages 6 and 7.

Be careful when using hot water as it may scald.

Conduct the investigation accurately and fairly by ensuring that the thermometer used is the same for each surface, the distance from the surface is the same and the starting temperature is the same in each case. Take the same number of readings over the same time period and intervals.

Leslie's cube

A Leslie's cube is commonly used in schools to demonstrate how the nature of a surface affects the rate at which thermal energy is absorbed or emitted.

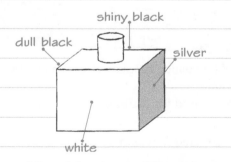

shiny black

dull black

silver

white

Four of its sides have different natures, as shown.

Now try this

1 Sketch four curves on a temperature–time graph for the four sides of a Leslie's cube that has been filled with hot water. **(4 marks)**

2 Explain why the starting temperature for the Leslie's cube practical needs to be kept constant. **(4 marks)**

Dangers and uses

The amount of **energy** that is transferred by an electromagnetic wave is dependent on its **wavelength** or **frequency**. The **highest frequencies** (shortest wavelengths) are the most energetic and the **most dangerous** waves.

Gamma-rays are emitted due to changes in the nucleus of an atom.

Dangers

X-rays and gamma-rays can cause **mutations** (changes) to the DNA in cells in the body. This may kill the cells or cause **cancer.**

UV in sunlight can damage skin cells, causing **sunburn**. Over time, exposure to UV can cause **skin cancer**. UV can also damage the **eyes** leading to eye conditions.

Infrared radiation transfers thermal energy. Too much infrared radiation can cause **skin burns.**

Microwaves heat water – so they can heat the water inside our bodies. Heating cells can damage or kill them.

high frequency

- gamma-rays
- X-rays
- ultraviolet
- visible light
- infrared
- microwaves
- radio waves

low frequency

Uses

- to sterilise food and medical equipment
- in scanners to detect cancer
- to treat cancer

- to look inside objects, including medical X-rays to look inside bodies
- in airport security scanners, to see what people have in their luggage

- to detect security marks made using special pens
- inside fluorescent lamps
- to detect forged banknotes (real banknotes have markings that glow in UV light)
- to disinfect water

- allows us to see, lights up rooms and streets, buildings and roads (illumination)
- photography

- in cooking (by grills and toasters)
- to make thermal images (images using heat), used by police and rescue services
- in short-range communications, such as between laptops or other small computers
- in remote controls for TVs and other appliances, where the signal only has to travel short distances
- to send information along optical fibres
- in security systems such as burglar alarms, to detect people moving around

- in mobile phones, and to communicate by satellite transmissions
- for cooking (in microwave ovens)

- broadcasting radio and TV programmes
- communicating with ships, aeroplanes and satellites

Worked example

State which types of electromagnetic radiation are:

(a) used for cooking   **(2 marks)**
microwave and infrared

(b) used for cleaning things   **(2 marks)**
ultraviolet and gamma-rays

(c) most dangerous.   **(3 marks)**
ultraviolet, X-rays and gamma-rays

Radiation dose

Radiation dose is a measure of the risk of harm to the human body due to the body being exposed to harmful radiation.

The effect that ultraviolet rays, X-rays and gamma-rays have on the body depends on the radiation type and size of dose.

Radiation dose is measured in sieverts (Sv) or millisieverts (mSv). We are exposed to much less than 1 mSv from background radiation. A dose of 1 Sv is high and could lead to death.

Now try this

1 Describe how X-rays are useful to doctors but can also be harmful to patients.   **(3 marks)**
2 Describe the differences in how microwaves and infrared radiation cook food.   **(5 marks)**
3 Describe how different types of electromagnetic radiation can be harmful to humans.   **(4 marks)**

Lenses

A lens forms an image by refracting light. The nature of the images formed by convex lenses and concave lenses can be shown by drawing ray diagrams.

Lenses and refraction

Lenses use refraction to bend light. There are two main types of lens – **convex** and **concave**.

Lenses that are thicker in the middle are **convex** lenses and those that are thinner in the middle are **concave** lenses.

convex lens

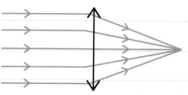

A convex lens bends rays of light towards one another, bringing them to a point.

concave lens

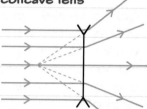

A concave lens bends rays of light away from each other.

Focal length and principal focus

Light is brought to a focus by a convex lens at the **principal focus**. The distance from the centre of the lens to the principal focus is called the focal length of the lens.

Parallel rays of light all converge to pass through f.

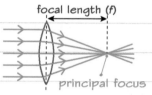
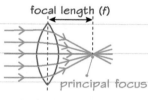

The thicker lens on the right refracts the light more than the thinner lens on the left, so it has a shorter focal length.

Parallel rays of light diverge so that they all seem to come from f.

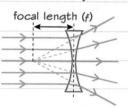
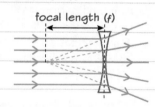

The thinner lens on the right has a longer focal length than the thick lens on the left.

Worked example

Draw ray diagrams to show (a) a convex lens with a short focal length and (b) a convex lens with a long focal length. **(4 marks)**

(a)   (b)

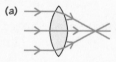
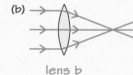

lens a   lens b

The thicker lens bends light more than the thinner lens, so it has a shorter focal length. You could also change the focal length by changing the type of glass that the lens is made from.

Real and virtual images

- A real image is formed where light rays converge and are actually focused on a screen. Real images can be formed by convex lenses.
- A virtual image is formed by light rays that appear to come from a point, but do not actually do so.
- Concave lenses always form a virtual image. A convex lens will form a virtual image if the object is placed between the lens and its principal focus.

Now try this

1 Describe the images produced by (a) convex and (b) concave lenses. **(2 marks)**

2 Describe the factors that could affect the focal length of a lens. **(2 marks)**

3 Describe how a virtual image is different from a real image. **(2 marks)**

Real and virtual images

The images produced by a lens depend on the **type of lens** being used and the **position of the object** with respect to the lens.

Real images and magnification

Convex lenses can produce real images of different sizes. As the object gets closer to the lens, the image size increases. A real image will not be produced by a convex lens when it is closer to the lens than the focal point. The ratio of the size of the image compared with the size of the object is called the magnification. Magnification is calculated using:

$$\text{magnification} = \frac{\text{image height}}{\text{object height}}$$

Magnification has no units. The image and object height should be measured either both in cm or both in mm.

> A magnification greater than one means that the image is larger than the object.
> A magnification less than one means that the image is smaller than the object.

The nature of a real image

Far from the lens, the real image is upside down and smaller than the object.

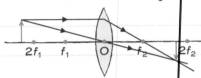

Moving the object closer to the lens causes the image to become larger. The position of the image will move away from the lens but will remain real and upside down.

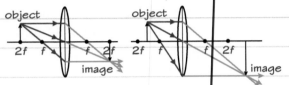

At a distance of twice the focal length (2f), the object and image are the same size. Between f and 2f, the image is magnified.

Virtual images

A **virtual image** is formed by a convex lens when the object is between the focal point and the lens.

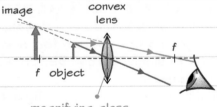

magnifying glass

The virtual image produced by a convex lens has an image height greater than the object height, which means the magnification will be greater than 1.

A concave lens always produces a virtual image.

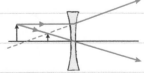
object outside focal point

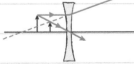
object inside focal point

The image height produced by a concave lens is smaller than the object height, so the magnification will be less than 1.

Worked example

A convex lens is used to produce a virtual image. The image height is 12 cm and the object height is 4 cm.
(a) Describe how the virtual image is formed.
(2 marks)

The object is placed closer to the lens than the principal focus, so the rays diverge to form a virtual image from where the rays of light appear to come, but do not actually do so.

(b) Calculate the magnification of the image.
(2 marks)

magnification = image height ÷ object height
= 12 cm ÷ 4 cm = 3

Now try this

1 A convex lens of focal length 4 cm is used to form an image of an object that is 5 cm high, placed 12 cm away from the lens.
(a) Draw a ray diagram for this arrangement.
(4 marks)
(b) Describe the image formed. **(3 marks)**
(c) Calculate the magnification of the image based on the ray diagram that you have drawn.
(2 marks)

Visible light

The wavelengths of visible light can be reflected, absorbed or transmitted.

Specular reflection

Specular reflection occurs when waves are reflected from a smooth surface.

When parallel rays of light are incident on a **smooth**, plane surface such as a mirror, the reflected light rays will also be **parallel**.

The sizes of any irregularities on the surface are much smaller than the wavelength of the wave.

Diffuse reflection

Diffuse reflection occurs when the surface is **not smooth** and has rough irregularities. The size of the irregularities is comparable with the wavelength of the wave. The incident wave is then reflected at **many different angles** and the reflected rays will not be parallel, such as when light is reflected off a painted wall. Diffuse reflection from a rough surface is also called **scattering**.

The colour spectrum

Visible light makes up a very small part of the electromagnetic spectrum. What we see can be split into different colours by a prism.

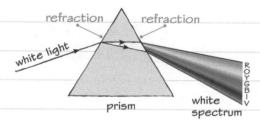

These colours all have a different wavelength, ranging from the longest wavelength at the red end of the spectrum to the shortest wavelength at the violet end.

Differential absorption at surfaces

The colour of an opaque object appears based on how the

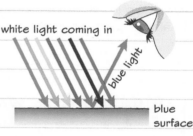

atoms at its surface respond to the light being shone on them. A material appears blue because its atoms reflect the blue wavelengths and absorb all of the others. A body that absorbs all wavelengths of visible light incident on it will appear black.

Filters

Filters let through different colours of light and absorb all other colours. For example, a green filter will let through or 'transmit' green light and absorb all of the other wavelengths.

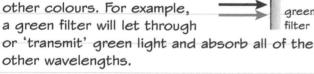

A transparent material such as glass will transmit all the light incident on it without it being absorbed. A translucent material such as frosted glass will transmit some light but scatter most of it.

Worked example

(a) Explain which type of reflection you would associate with a plane mirror or a calm lake surface. **(2 marks)**

specular reflection, because the surface is smooth, so parallel rays or wavefronts that are incident on these surfaces will be reflected as parallel rays or wavefronts

(b) Explain what happens to white light when it hits an opaque white surface. **(3 marks)**

The opaque surface will not transmit visible light, but will absorb or reflect the white light because it reflects all wavelengths equally.

Now try this

1 State which type of reflection you would associate with a gravel path. **(1 mark)**

2 Describe how a filter works to let through red light. **(2 marks)**

3 Explain what you would see when white light travels through a red filter and then a green filter. **(2 marks)**

Black body radiation

All bodies or objects above absolute zero of temperature will emit and absorb infrared radiation. The hotter the body, the more infrared radiation it will emit in a given time.

Emitting radiation

A hot cup of tea at 90°C will emit radiation that is mainly in the **infrared part** of the EM spectrum, whereas the Sun's surface temperature of 5700°C means that it emits **visible light** and **ultraviolet** radiation which have a shorter wavelength than infrared. Bodies that are much hotter than the Sun will emit **X-rays**.

A perfect black body is an object that absorbs all the radiation that is incident on it. A black body will not reflect or transmit any radiation incident on it. A perfect black body is also a perfect emitter of radiation.

Factors affecting temperature

1 A body at a constant temperature absorbs the same amount of radiation as it emits.

2 An object will increase its temperature if it absorbs more radiation than it emits.

3 An object will decrease its temperature if it emits more radiation than it absorbs.

As the temperature of a body increases, more energetic radiation is emitted, including infrared, visible and UV.

Intensity and wavelength

Intensity is the energy emitted per square metre per second – or the power emitted per square metre. The intensity and wavelength of the radiation emitted by a body depend on its temperature. As the object gets hotter, the intensity increases and the wavelength that corresponds to the maximum intensity decreases.

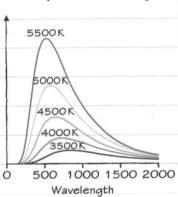

Worked example

Suggest why the colour of a star depends on its surface temperature.

(4 marks)

Temperature is related to wavelength. The wavelength of electromagnetic radiation in the visible part of the EM spectrum determines the colour that is seen so changing the temperature changes the wavelength, which changes the colour.

Now try this

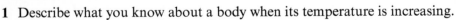

1 Describe what you know about a body when its temperature is increasing. **(2 marks)**

2 Which body will emit the most radiation? Select one answer.
   A   A cup of tea in a white cup at 90 °C.
   B   A cup of tea in a black cup at 90 °C.
   C   A cup of tea in a silver cup at 90 °C.
   D   A cup of tea in a black cup at 80 °C. **(1 mark)**

3 Explain why perfect absorbers and emitters of radiation are called black bodies. **(2 marks)**

Extended response – Waves

There will be at least one 6-mark question on your exam paper. For these questions, you will need to think scientifically and structure your answer logically, showing how the points you make are related to each other. You can revise the topics for this question, which is about **waves**, on pages 74–86.

Worked example

Exposure to certain types of electromagnetic radiation can have harmful effects on the human body.

Describe how exposure to electromagnetic radiation can be harmful.

Your answer should refer to the types of electromagnetic radiation and the damage that they may cause. **(6 marks)**

long wavelength, low frequency

short wavelength, high frequency

radio waves   microwaves   infrared   visible light   ultraviolet   X-rays   gamma-rays

Apart from radio waves and visible light, which are not deemed to cause damage to humans, the other five members of the electromagnetic spectrum do cause harmful effects.

Microwaves are absorbed by water molecules and can lead to internal heating of body cells, which can be harmful. Infrared radiation can cause burns to the skin.

Ultraviolet radiation can damage the eyes, leading to eye conditions. It can also cause skin cancer as surface cells are affected. X-rays and gamma-rays can both lead to cellular damage and mutations, which can lead to diseases such as cancer.

The initial sentence states which types of electromagnetic wave are dangerous and which are not. This will help to structure the rest of the answer.

Two of the low-energy members of the electromagnetic spectrum are commented on next.

The three higher-energy electromagnetic waves are then commented on. The energy of electromagnetic radiation is related directly to its frequency, so, as frequency increases, so does the energy and so does the extent of the damage.

UV, X-rays and gamma-rays are examples of **ionising radiation**. This can lead to tissue damage and possible mutations in cells. Although not mentioned here, you could be asked a question that relates specifically to the dangers of ionising radiation. Of the three types mentioned here, only gamma-rays come from the nucleus of the atom. You can read more about this on page 39.

Command word: Describe

When you are asked to **describe** something, you need to write down facts, events or processes accurately.

Now try this

Describe how the electromagnetic spectrum is useful to humans. Refer to specific members of the EM spectrum in your answer.

(6 marks)

Magnets and magnetic fields

Certain materials can be magnetised to become permanent or induced magnets.

Magnets and magnetic fields

Like magnetic poles **repel**. **Unlike** magnetic poles **attract**.

The magnetic field is strongest at the poles. The field lines are shown to be closer together and more concentrated. The magnetic field gets weaker the further you are from the poles.

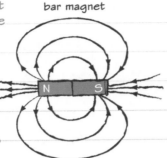

bar magnet

Magnetic field lines are always from N to S.

When two magnets are brought close together they will exert a force on each other. Like poles will repel and unlike poles will attract. This happens via the non-contact force of magnetism.

Permanent and induced magnets

- A permanent magnet produces its own magnetic field.
- An induced magnet is a material that will become a magnet when it is placed in a magnetic field.

Induced magnetism always causes a force of attraction. For example, iron paper clips can be attracted by a permanent magnet even though the paper clips are not permanent magnets. When removed from the magnetic field an induced magnet loses all or most of its magnetism immediately.

At room temperature, magnetic materials are made from iron, cobalt, nickel or steel.

Uses of magnets

Permanent	Induced
fridge magnets	electromagnets
compasses	circuit breakers
motors and generators	electric bells
loudspeakers	magnetic relays
door closers on fridges	

Plotting compasses

A plotting compass contains a small bar magnet. The Earth has a magnetic field and the compass needle will point in the direction of the Earth's magnetic field.

The direction of the magnetic field at any point is given by the direction of the force that would act on a north pole that is placed at that point in the field. The behaviour of the compass needle is evidence that the Earth's core is magnetic.

Worked example

What will the plotting compass needle look like when it is placed at point 1? **(1 mark)**

☐ ➡
☑ ➘
☐ ⬅
☐ ➡

Explain how you can tell if a magnetic material is a permanent or an induced magnet. **(2 marks)**

Induced magnetic material will always be attracted by a magnet, but a permanent magnet can be both attracted and repelled.

Induced magnets don't always have north and south poles. They can be thought of as always being magnetic but not always being magnets. North and south poles are sometimes called north-seeking and south-seeking poles.

Now try this

1 Draw the field lines for:
   (a) a weak bar magnet **(2 marks)**
   (b) a strong bar magnet. **(2 marks)**

2 Explain why unmagnetised iron is always attracted by a permanent magnet. **(3 marks)**

Current and magnetism

An **electric current** will create a **magnetic field**. The **shape, direction** and **strength** of the field depend on a number of factors.

The magnetic field around a long straight conductor

The shape of the magnetic field around a long straight conductor can be thought of as a series of concentric circles.

Be careful! Do not confuse the direction of the current with electron flow. You need to use the direction of conventional current which is taken to be from + to –.

B

The strength of the magnetic field depends on:
* the size of the current in the wire: it is directly proportional to the current
* the distance from the wire: it is inversely proportional to the distance from the wire.

The direction of the magnetic field depends on the direction of the electric current in the conductor.

If you point the thumb of your right hand in the direction of the flow of conventional current, the direction that your fingers curl will be the direction of the magnetic field.

The solenoid

A solenoid is a long coil of conducting wire, covered in insulating material. When a current flows through the solenoid, a strong magnetic field is produced inside the coil and a weaker magnetic field is produced around the coil. Solenoids are used in devices to produce large magnetic fields.

Shaping a long wire into a solenoid leads to a much stronger, uniform field inside the coil of the solenoid. This can be made stronger by inserting an iron bar. Electromagnets are solenoids with iron cores. The magnetic field is similar in shape to that of a bar magnet.

Worked example

Explain how the strength of a magnetic field due to a current in a long straight wire changes when:
(a) the current increases **(1 mark)**
It will increase.
(b) the distance increases. **(1 mark)**
It will decrease.

Maths skills **Directly proportional** means that as **one variable increases** the other **variable increases** at **the same rate.** If the current doubles, the magnetic field strength will also double.

Maths skills **Inversely proportional** means that as **one variable increases** the other **decreases**. If the distance doubles, the field strength halves.

Now try this

1 Draw the magnetic field around a wire when the current is flowing downwards. **(2 marks)**
2 The current flowing in a long straight wire and the distance from the wire are both doubled. Explain what effect this will have on the magnetic field strength. **(3 marks)**
3 Suggest how the magnetic field strength inside a solenoid could be increased. **(3 marks)**

Extended response – Magnetism and electromagnetism

There will be at least one 6-mark question on your exam paper. For these questions, you will need to think scientifically and structure your answer logically, showing how the points you make are related to each other. You can revise the topics for this question, which is about **magnetism** and **electromagnetism**, on pages 88 and 89.

Worked example

A wire is arranged vertically as shown, with plotting compasses placed around it.

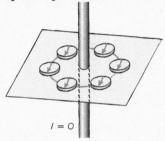

I = 0

Explain what happens once a current starts to flow in the wire.

Your answer should refer to what happens when the current, and the distance of the plotting compasses from the wire, are changed, and how the size of the magnetic field would change if measured with a meter. **(6 marks)**

At first, there is no current flowing in the wire, and the plotting compass needles all point in the same direction because they are aligned with the Earth's magnetic field.

When a current flows in a long straight wire, a circular magnetic field is produced around the wire and the compass needles will re-align to point in a circular direction. This will be clockwise if the current is in one direction and will be anticlockwise if the direction of the current is reversed.

The magnetic field will be stronger if the current is increased, and it will be stronger closer to the wire, and get smaller the further away from the wire you go.

Command word: Explain

When you are asked to **explain** something, it is not enough to just state or describe something. Your answer **must** contain some reasoning or justification of the points you make based on the appropriate physics. This needs to be communicated clearly using good spelling, punctuation and grammar.

> The answer starts by stating how the compass needles are behaving before any current flows in the wire.

> The answer then mentions that a magnetic effect is caused by the current, leading to a circular magnetic field around the wire.

> The answer then mentions how changing the current and the distance affects the strength of the magnetic field.

Now try this

Magnetism can be used to attract a variety of materials of different masses. Explain how the strength of the magnetic field can be changed to make this possible. Your answer should refer to how the size of the magnetic field strength can be changed **with** and **without** the use of an **electric current**. **(6 marks)**

The Solar System

The Solar System contains the Sun, the eight planets, dwarf planets, and the natural satellites or moons that orbit the planets.

The Solar System

You need to remember the order of the eight planets, going from the Sun.

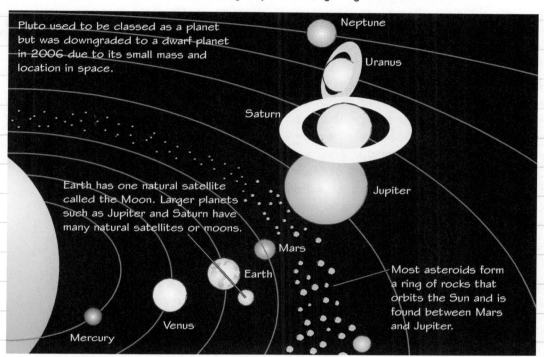

Pluto used to be classed as a planet but was downgraded to a dwarf planet in 2006 due to its small mass and location in space.

Neptune

Uranus

Saturn

Jupiter

Earth has one natural satellite called the Moon. Larger planets such as Jupiter and Saturn have many natural satellites or moons.

Mars

Earth

Most asteroids form a ring of rocks that orbits the Sun and is found between Mars and Jupiter.

Venus

Mercury

The Milky Way

The Solar System may appear large to us, but it is only a very small part of the Milky Way – a galaxy of over one billion stars. Our Solar System is situated in one of the spiral arms of the Milky Way.

Formation of the Sun

- The Sun, like every other star, was formed when a nebula (a cloud of dust and gas) was pulled together by the force of gravitational attraction.
- The size of a star depends on the mass of dust and gas that is in the nebula when the star starts to form. Very heavy stars come from very heavy nebulae.
- Our Sun is an average star, of fairly average mass and brightness. It will have been formed from a small nebula.

Worked example

(a) State what the parts of the Solar System are. **(3 marks)**

The Solar System is composed of the Sun, eight planets, dwarf planets, and the natural satellites (moons) that orbit the planets.

(b) Describe how stars form and why they have different masses. **(3 marks)**

A star forms when a cloud of dust and gas, called a nebula, is pulled together by the force of gravitational attraction. Very massive stars are formed from very high-mass nebulae, whereas low-mass stars like the Sun are formed from the dust and gas in low-mass nebulae.

Now try this

 1 Name the planets in order from the Sun, starting with the furthest. **(2 marks)**

 2 Suggest why some planets have been discovered more recently than others. **(3 marks)**

 3 Suggest the similarities and differences between how stars form and how planets form. **(3 marks)**

The life cycle of stars

Stars go through a number of **stages** in their lives. Their eventual **fate** depends on their **mass**.

Low-mass stars

The Sun was formed about 4.6 billion years ago and is nearly halfway through its life. Stars with masses up to four times the mass of the Sun are classified as low-mass stars.

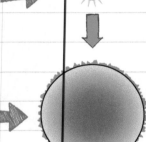

1 The cloud of **dust** and **hydrogen gas** (a **nebula**) is pulled inwards by the force of gravity. As the dust and gas contracts the nebular gets hotter since work is being done on it.

2 Eventually, the dust and gas become hot enough for the hydrogen nuclei to fuse. **Nuclear fusion** leads to heavier **helium nuclei** being produced and large amounts of **energy** being released. The star will begin to give out **light** and is now a **main-sequence** star. Stars are main-sequence stars for most of their lives. Fusion reactions lead to an equilibrium between the gravitational collapse of a star and the expansion of a star due to fusion energy.

3 When most of the hydrogen gas has been converted to helium, the star will **expand** and become a **red giant**. When the core of this star collapses, other **heavier elements** are formed.

4 Eventually, all nuclear fusion stops due to the elements that cause fusion being used up, and the star **collapses** to become a **white dwarf**.

5 The white dwarf cools and stops glowing to become a black dwarf.

High-mass stars

A star with a much higher mass than the Sun follows the same first stages of the life cycle, but each stage is shorter. When most of its hydrogen is used up it forms a **red supergiant**. At the end of this stage the star will explode as

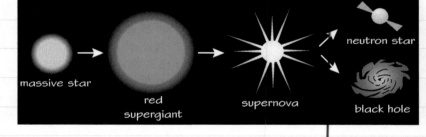

massive star

red supergiant

supernova

neutron star

black hole

a **supernova**. If what remains after the explosion is less than four times the mass of the Sun it will be pulled together by gravity to form a very small, dense star called a **neutron star**. More massive remnants form **black holes**.

Fusion processes in stars produce all of the naturally occurring elements. Elements heavier than iron are produced in supernova explosions, and then distributed throughout the Universe.

Worked example

Describe how the fate of a low-mass star is different from that of a high-mass star. **(6 marks)**

A low-mass star will move off the main sequence and expand to become a red giant, then cool and contract to become a white dwarf. A high-mass star will move off the main sequence, become a red supergiant and explode in a supernova. The mass left in the core will become a very dense neutron star or a black hole.

Now try this

1 State the stages in the life cycle of:
   (a) low-mass stars **(4 marks)**
   (b) high-mass stars. **(4 marks)**
2 Explain why the temperature of a white dwarf increases at first despite it losing thermal energy. **(2 marks)**
3 Explain the roles of gravity and thermal expansion in the stages of a star's life cycle. **(4 marks)**

Satellites and orbits

Gravity provides the force that allows planets, natural satellites and artificial satellites to stay in their circular orbits.

Natural satellites

Natural satellites were formed by natural processes. Examples include:

- the eight **planets** in the Solar System which orbit the Sun
- the **moons** which orbit planets in the Solar System.

Artificial satellites

Artificial satellites are manufactured and have been launched into space from Earth using rockets. Examples include:

- satellites in **geostationary orbits** around the Earth being used for global positioning satellite (GPS) systems
- satellites in **low polar orbits** around the Earth being used for weather monitoring, military, spying or Earth observation purposes
- satellites **sent from Earth** to orbit and monitor the Sun, other planets or asteroids in the Solar System.

Circular orbits

Artificial satellites orbiting the Earth, and planets orbiting the Sun, tend to move in circular or near-circular orbits.

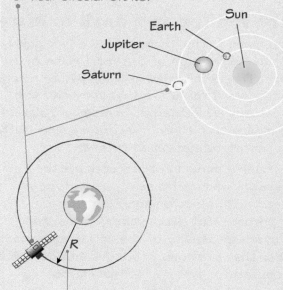

The gravitational force acting on a body in a circular orbit will be the same at each point of the orbit, since the radius is fixed. The speed of the orbit will not change, but the velocity will be constantly changing because the direction is constantly changing.

Planets, moons and artificial satellites

- **Satellites** are bodies of smaller mass that move in paths around bodies of greater mass.
- **Planets** in our Solar System move in near-circular orbits around the Sun. The mass of the Sun is much greater than any of the planets in our Solar System.
- **Moons** (smaller masses) move in near-circular orbits around planets (larger masses). Moons are natural satellites.
- **Artificial satellites** are much less massive than the moons of planets, and can be made to orbit planets or moons in circular paths.

Worked example

Compare the motion of Earth, Jupiter and Saturn as they orbit the Sun. **(3 marks)**

All three planets travel in circular orbits and have a constant speed and a changing velocity. As the distance from the Sun increases, the orbital speed decreases. The Earth has a higher orbital speed than Jupiter which has a higher orbital speed than Saturn.

Now try this

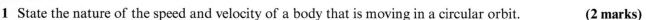

1 State the nature of the speed and velocity of a body that is moving in a circular orbit. **(2 marks)**
2 State what provides the force that causes planets, moons and artificial satellites to move in circular orbits. **(1 mark)**
3 Describe how natural satellites and artificial satellites are:
  (a) similar **(2 marks)**
  (b) different. **(2 marks)**

Red-shift

Red-shift is the observed increase in the wavelength of the light from distant galaxies that supports the Big Bang theory.

Red-shift

A light source moving away from an observer will have a **greater wavelength** and a **lower frequency**. It is 'red-shifted'.

A light source moving towards an observer will have a **smaller wavelength** and a **higher frequency**. It is 'blue-shifted'.

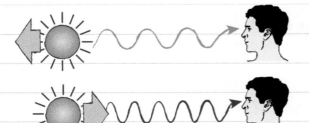

Big Bang theory

- The Big Bang theory suggests that our Universe is around 13.8 billion years old and started from a very small region that was incredibly hot and dense.
- Since 1998 observations of supernovae suggest that distant galaxies are receding faster than originally thought. This discovery is causing astronomers some confusion.
- Scientists now believe that some unknown source of energy, called **dark energy**, must be causing this accelerating motion. The force of gravity cannot be used by itself to explain dark energy, because gravity is an attractive force, so it should actually be slowing them down.

Red-shift and evidence for the expanding Universe

In 1929, the astronomer Edwin Hubble discovered that the light reaching Earth from galaxies was red-shifted. He found this out by looking at the spectral lines in the absorption spectra of stars that are moving away from us.

Galaxy b's lines are red-shifted the most, so it is moving away from us the fastest.

laboratory hydrogen spectral lines	blue ... red
galaxy a spectral lines	blue ... red
galaxy b spectral lines	blue ... red

Dark matter and dark energy

Astronomers think that the stars in a galaxy make a tiny fraction of the total mass of a galaxy. They know that galaxies would rotate much faster if the stars that they can see and detect were the only matter in galaxies. This means that there must be missing matter that cannot be detected or seen.

The missing mass is called dark matter because it cannot be seen, as it does not interact with electromagnetic radiation. The presence of dark matter means that the average density of the universe is much bigger than previously thought and cannot be accounted for just by 'normal matter'.

Worked example

Explain how red-shift suggests that the Universe is expanding. **(4 marks)**

The light received on Earth from most galaxies is red-shifted. This means that most galaxies are moving away from us. The furthest galaxies from us have the greatest red-shift, so are moving away from us faster. This suggests that the Universe is expanding.

Now try this

1 Define red-shift. **(2 marks)**

2 State the observations that led astronomers to propose the idea of dark energy. **(2 marks)**

3 Explain why red-shift, on its own, is not sufficiently firm evidence to suggest that the Big Bang occurred. **(3 marks)**

2 Wood has been readily available (**1**) for thousands of years (**1**) and has not had to be discovered or mined, or have any extra technology developed (e.g. nuclear reactors / power stations) in order for it to be used to produce thermal energy (**1**).

10. Extended response – Energy

*Answer could include the following points (for all **6 marks**, two advantages and two disadvantages with good supporting explanation should be supplied):

- advantages of wind – renewable, no fuel needed, no carbon dioxide gas emissions
- disadvantages – unsightly, unreliable
- advantages of coal – efficient, reliable
- disadvantages – non-renewable, carbon dioxide and sulfur dioxide gas emissions.

11. Circuit symbols

1 filament lamp (**1**), LED (**1**)

2 circuit to contain a cell (**1**), lamp (**1**), LDR (**1**)

3 ammeters in series (**1**), voltmeters in parallel (**1**)

12. Electrical charge and current

1 current: ampere (**1**); charge: coulomb (**1**)

2 $Q = I\,t = 0.25\,\text{A} \times (60 \times 60)\,\text{s}$ (**1**) $= 900$ (**1**) C (**1**)

3 $Q = I\,t$ so $t = Q \div I$ (**1**) $= 30\,000\,\text{C} \div 0.25\,\text{A}$ (**1**) $= 120\,000$ (**1**) s (**1**)

13. Current, resistance and potential difference

1 $V = I\,R = 3.2\,\text{A} \times 18\,\Omega$ (**1**) $= 57.6$ (**1**) V (**1**)

2 $R = V\,I = 28\,\text{V} \div 0.4\,\text{A}$ (**1**) $= 70$ (**1**) Ω (**1**)

14. Required practical – Investigating resistance

1 Repeating results allows you to check for similar results (**1**) between two sets of readings and allows you to determine the precision (**1**) of the data. You can see if there are any anomalies (**1**). The data are more reliable if the same values or patterns are obtained more than once (**1**).

2 When resistors are added in series, the current has only one route to travel down (**1**), so it has to go through all three resistors and the resistance is higher (**1**). When resistors are arranged in parallel, there are more routes for the current to travel down – the current splits (**1**) and so only has to go through one resistor, and the resistance is lower (**1**).

3 Any four from: Variable resistor allows a range of results to be collected for V and I (**1**) so that a graph of resistance against length can be plotted (**1**) and a relationship can be determined (**1**). Switch allows current to be switched off so that wire cools (**1**) and more accurate results for resistance can be obtained (**1**) / safety issue (**1**).

15. Resistors

(a) graph of S-shaped curve through origin of I against V for filament lamp (**1**), labelled axes (**1**)

(b) As the current goes up, the temperature goes up (**1**) and, as the temperature goes up, the resistance goes up (**1**) and the gradient goes down (**1**).

16. LDRs and thermistors

1 (a) temperature (**1**)

(b) light intensity (**1**)

2 Provide an example of a circuit where temperature (**1**) and light intensity (**1**) vary their resistances (**1**) to turn on an output device (**1**). The marks can be awarded only if the

operation of the circuit is explained in terms of changing light levels and temperature. An example would be for a circuit that turns a light / heater on or off in a greenhouse.

17. Required practical – Investigating I–V characteristics

1 As the pd increases across the filament lamp, the current through the filament lamp also increases (**1**) and, as current increases, the energy dissipated as thermal energy increases, leading to more vibrations of the metal ions in the filament (**1**), which increases the resistance of the lamp (**1**). So the current increases by less and less per unit increase in pd (**1**), leading to a graph of decreasing gradient as the pd gets bigger and bigger (**1**).

2 The diode allows current to flow through it in one direction only (**1**) and does not allow current to flow in the opposite direction (**1**). It requires a certain potential difference before a current starts to flow through it (**1**).

3 Resistance is given by $R = V \div I$ (**1**). The gradient of the graph is $I \div V$ (**1**) so the resistance is the inverse of the gradient (**1**).

18. Series and parallel circuits

1 Current will stop flowing in series if one bulb breaks (**1**) so parallel arrangement used so that lights stay on (**1**) if one or more bulbs break (**1**).

2 More bulbs in parallel means a higher current (**1**) is drawn from the cell, so finite amount of stored chemical energy (**1**) decreases (**1**) more rapidly (**1**).

3 (a) 40 (**1**) Ω (**1**)

(b) $I = V \div R = 12\,\text{V} \div 40\,\Omega$ (**1**) $= 0.3$ (**1**) A (**1**)

19. ac and dc

1 (a) any three devices, e.g. remote controls, torches, mobile phones, calculators, watches (**1 mark each**)

(b) any three mains-operated devices, e.g. electric oven, microwave oven, fridge, freezer, tumble dryer, hairdryer, TV (**1 mark each**)

2 (a) They both transfer energy (**1**)

(b) Potential difference in ac alternates (**1**) but in dc it is constant (**1**).

20. Mains electricity

1 (a) brown (**1**), (b) blue (**1**), (c) yellow and green (**1**)

2 Live wire touches metal case (**1**), earth wire forms circuit with live wire and pulls a large current through the fuse (**1**), large current melts fuse and isolates appliance (**1**), device now at 0 V and no longer dangerous to user (**1**).

3 Current enters the plug through the live wire (**1**) and this forms a circuit with the neutral wire (**1**). The earth wire becomes part of the circuit only if the live wire comes loose and touches the metal casing / part of the appliance to which the earth wire is connected (**1**).

21. Electrical power

1 $P = E \div t = 400\,000\,\text{J} \div (200\,\text{s})$ (**1**) $= 2000$ (**1**) W (**1**)

2 $I = P \div V = 3000\,\text{W} \div 230\,\text{V}$ (**1**) $= 13$ (**1**) A (**1**)

3 $P = I^2 R$, so $= \sqrt{P \div R}$ (**1**) $= \sqrt{2000\,\text{W} \div 470\,\Omega}$ (**1**) $= 2.1$ or 2.06 (**1**) A (**1**)

22. Electrical energy

1 $E = Q\,V = 24\,\text{C} \times 6\,\text{V}$ (**1**) $= 144$ (**1**) J (**1**)

2 $V = E \div Q$ (**1**) so as unit of energy is J and charge is C (**1**) we get 1 V = 1 J/C (**1**)

3 $E = Q\,V$, so $Q = E \div V = 2800\,\text{J} \div 14\,\text{V}$ (**1**) $= 200$ (**1**) C (**1**)

23. The National Grid

1. (a) The National Grid is a system of wires (**1**) and transformers (**1**).
   (b) transmitting electrical energy / power (**1**) from power stations to homes, factories, etc. across the UK (**1**)
2. Step-up transformers at power stations step up voltage (**1**) and decrease current (**1**) for efficient transmission of electrical energy across the UK. Step-down transformers at substations step down voltage and increase current (**1**) for use in homes and factories (**1**).

24. Static electricity

1. (a) negatively charged (**1**)
   (b) positively charged (**1**)
2. a positively charged duster and a negatively charged rod (**1**)
3. Protons are held in the nucleus (**1**) by strong forces (**1**) so too much energy would be required (**1**) to transfer them.
4. Polythene is rubbed and becomes negatively charged (**1**) as it gains electrons; opposite charges attract (**1**) so the suspended rod will move towards the polythene (**1**) if positively charged.

25. Electric fields

1. (a) Greater mass means less acceleration (**1**) from $a = F / m$ (**1**)
   (b) It would move in the opposite direction (**1**) with the same initial acceleration (**1**).
2. An electric field is created in the region around a charged particle (**1**). If another charged particle is placed in (the region of) this electric field then it will experience a non-contact force (**1**), which will cause it to be attracted or repelled (**1**). Electrons (negatively charged) are attracted to the positive charge, which explains the phenomenon of static electricity (**1**).

26. Extended response – Electricity

*Answer could include the following points (**6**):
- arrange a suitable circuit, e.g. a circuit with a cell, switch, ammeter, voltmeter, space for component to be inserted
- take a number of readings for current and potential difference when the cell is arranged in one direction
- repeat the results for the current flowing in the opposite direction once the cell has been reversed
- plot a suitable graph, e.g. of current against pd
- compare the I–V graphs with those for a diode, resistor or filament lamp to see if it is one of those
- change the light intensity or temperature to see if the component may be a light-dependent resistor or a thermistor
- plot a suitable graph of resistance against length, light intensity or temperature.

27. Density

1. density = mass ÷ volume = 84 kg ÷ 0.075 m³ (**1**) = 1120 (**1**) kg/m³ (**1**)
2. mass = density × volume = 0.05 m³ × 2700 kg/m³ (**1**) = 135 (**1**) kg (**1**)

28. Required practical – Investigating density

1. density = mass ÷ volume = 454 g ÷ 256 cm³ (**1**) = 1.77 (**1**) g/cm³ (**1**)
2. Mass reading can be misread by human error, parallax error or systematic error (**1**); volume can be misread by parallax error or reading the top of the meniscus for water (**1**); a value that is too high for the mass (**1**) or too low for the volume will lead to a value that is too high for the density (**1**).

29. Changes of state

1. Thermal energy is transferred from the warmer room to the ice (**1**) and causes the ice to melt (**1**) and become 1.5 kg of liquid water (**1**).
2. A change in state can be reversed so that the material recovers its original properties, similar to a physical change (**1**), but a chemical change cannot be reversed (**1**).
3. Thermal energy is supplied to the copper metal, bonds are broken and it turns from a solid to a liquid at a constant temperature (**1**) once it reaches its melting point (**1**). Further heating of the liquid copper causes its temperature (**1**) to rise until it reaches its boiling point, at which point it turns from a liquid to a gas at a constant temperature (**1**). If the gaseous copper atoms continue to be heated then the temperature of the gas will increase (**1**).

30. Internal energy

1. A change in kinetic energy will lead to a change in the internal energy (**1**) of the system as well as a change in the temperature (**1**) of the material. If the total kinetic energy of the particles doubles, the absolute temperature of the material will also double (or similar argument / reverse argument) (**1**).
2. The internal energy will decrease (**1**) due to a lowering of temperature (**1**) caused by a decrease in the kinetic energy of the steel particles (**1**). As the steel turns from a liquid to a solid, the potential energy of the particles will also decrease as energy is lost to the surroundings and new bonds are formed (**1**).

31. Specific latent heat

1. $E = m L = 50$ kg $\times 334\,000$ J/kg (**1**) $= 16\,700\,000$ (**1**) J (**1**)
2. $E = m L = 25$ kg $\times 2\,260\,000$ J/kg (**1**) $= 56\,500\,000$ (**1**) J (**1**)

32. Particle motion in gases

1. Average kinetic energy of gas particles is related to temperature (**1**), so, as the temperature increases, the average kinetic energy will also increase (**1**).
2. (a) The average speed is slower (**1**).
   (b) The pressure is reduced (**1**) because there are fewer collisions / the particles do not hit the walls as hard (**1**).

33. Pressure in gases

1. $p_1 V_1 = p_2 V_2$ so $p_2 = (p_1 V_1) \div V_2$ (**1**) $= (200\,000$ Pa $\times 28$ cm³$) \div 44.8$ cm³ (**1**) $= 125\,000$ Pa (or 125 kPa) (**1**)
2. A gas compressed slowly (**1**) will change volume at a constant temperature because the thermal energy from the compression will be able to leave the system (**1**).
3. $p_1 V_1 = p_2 V_2$ so $V_2 = (p_1 V_1) \div p_2$ (**1**) $= (200$ kPa $\times 480$ m³$) \div 120$ kPa (**1**) $= 800$ (**1**) m³ (**1**)

34. Extended response – Particle model

*Answer could include the following points (**6**):
- Pressure is caused by moving particles colliding with the sides of a container.
- Pressure is force per unit area.
- Decreasing the volume of a gas quickly means that work is being done on the gas.
- When work is done on the gas the kinetic energy / speed of the particles increases.
- Faster-moving particles collide with the walls / area more frequently, leading to an increase in pressure.
- Increasing the temperature of a gas at constant volume means that the particles have greater kinetic energy and speed, and so collide more frequently with the area, so greater pressure.
- The internal energy of a gas is entirely kinetic.

35. The structure of the atom

1   The diameter of the atom is around 100 000 times greater than the diameter of a nucleus (**1**). The diameter of the nucleus on the poster will be around 60 cm ÷ 100 000 (**1**) or a diameter of about 6×10^{-4} (**1**) cm (**1**).

2   (a) Electrons gain energy (**1**) and can move to higher energy levels (**1**).

    (b) Electrons lose energy (**1**) and move down to lower energy levels (**1**).

36. Atoms, isotopes and ions

1   An isotope is an atom of the same element (so it has the same number of protons) (**1**) with a different number of neutrons in its nuclei (**1**).

2   Atoms of an element contain the same number of protons as electrons (**1**) and have a neutral charge overall (**1**), whereas ions of an element have the same number of protons but can gain electrons so that they have a negative charge (more electrons than protons) (**1**) or lose electrons so that they have a positive charge (more protons than electrons) (**1**).

3   Electrons are in fixed energy levels in the shells of atoms / orbiting the nucleus (**1**). If electromagnetic radiation of the same / more energy as the electron energy level is absorbed, then the electron will be able to leave the atom and the atom will become a positive ion (**1**). If the electromagnetic radiation does not have enough energy as the electron energy level, then the electron cannot leave and the atom does not become an ion (**1**). Since different atoms of different elements have different electron energy level values, some atoms will lose electrons and others will not (**1**).

37. Models of the atom

1   Positive alpha particles were fired at the nucleus (**1**). Most went through undeflected (**1**), so most of the atom must be empty space (**1**) and there is a small nucleus because only very few alpha particles bounced back (**1**).

2   Scientists suggest ideas or hypotheses (**1**) that then need to be investigated / tested by experiment (**1**). If the evidence / data suggest that the new model explains the data / observations better than the old model then the new model will replace the old model (**1**), provided that scientists agree based on identical repeat findings that validate the evidence and the new model (**1**).

38. Radioactive decay

1   (a) the number of radioactive decays / particles emitted from an unstable nucleus (**1**) per second (**1**)

    (b) becquerel (Bq) (**1**)

2   It decreases / goes down (**1**).

3   It increases (**1**) due to excess energy being lost through the emission of radioactive particles (**1**).

39. Nuclear radiation

1   neutrons, gamma-rays, beta particles, alpha particles (**1**)

2   You cannot predict (**1**) when a nucleus will decay by emitting radiation (**1**).

3   Alpha particles are highly ionising (**1**) and readily absorbed by nearby cells, which can lead to mutations (**1**) when inside the body. Outside the body they have a very short range and are unlikely to reach the body and cause harm to cells (**1**).

40. Uses of nuclear radiation

1   any three of: sterilising surgical equipment, killing cancer cells, preserving fruit, smoke alarms, thickness testing, X-ray films, etc. (**1 mark for each**)

2   contains alpha particles (**1**) which have a short range in air (**1**) and cannot reach the body (**1**)

3   Alpha particles are highly ionising so they are the best type of radiation to ionise the air (**1**), so that there is a bigger difference in the current across the detector when smoke gets into it (**1**). As the alpha particles are absorbed by a few centimetres of air, they will not expose a person to ionising radiation (**1**).

41. Nuclear equations

1   (a) Mass goes down by 4, charge by 2 (**1**) because 4 particles (2 protons, 2 neutrons) are lost as an alpha particle (**1**) and 2 of these are protons, which are positively charged (**1**) so the daughter nucleus has a nuclear charge that is 2 less than the parent nucleus.

    (b) Mass does not decrease, but nuclear charge of daughter nucleus increases by 1 (**1**) because the electron emitted as a beta particle has no / negligible mass (**1**) but a charge of -1 as a result of a neutron in the parent nucleus having changed to a proton (**1**).

2   $^{137}_{55}\text{Cs} \rightarrow \,^{137}_{56}\text{Ra} + \,^{0}_{1}\text{e}$ (**3**)

3   $^{232}_{90}\text{Th} \rightarrow \,^{228}_{88}\text{Ra} + \,^{4}_{2}\text{He}$ (**2**)

42. Half-life

1   120 Bq to 30 Bq is one-quarter of the activity or two half-lives in 4 hours (**1**) so one half-life is half of 4 hours, or 2 hours (**1**).

2   Any suitable pair of readings from the graph where the second activity is half the first, e.g. activity at 0 hours is 1100 Bq; 550 Bq is at 13 hours (**1**) so half-life is 13 hours (**1**).

43. Contamination and irradiation

1   Irradiation is exposure to radiation reaching the body from an external source (**1**); contamination is the eating, swallowing or breathing in of unwanted radioactive material (**1**).

2   Some sources of background radiation do not come into contact with the body such as cosmic rays from the Sun and medical X-rays (**1**), but other sources such as radon gas and radioisotopes in food are taken into the body (**1**).

44. Hazards of radiation

1   a short exposure time (**1**), as low a dose as possible (**1**) and the use of protective clothing (**1**) for those using radioactive sources on a regular basis

2   It is important for scientists to analyse or test other scientists' claims (**1**) to see if new knowledge or understanding of the area of science can be developed / improved for the benefit of science and people (**1**).

3   Ionising radiation ionises atoms (**1**) making them more reactive and allowing change to DNA to occur (**1**), whereas non-ionising radiation cannot do this because there is not enough energy to ionise atoms (**1**).

45. Background radiation

1   (a) The sector for radon would be much smaller (**1**).

    (b) The sector for radon would be bigger (**1**).

2   Radon gas emits alpha particles, which are highly ionising (**1**) and cause damage inside the body (**1**), but have too small a range in air to reach the body, so they will not cause harm (**1**).

46. Medical uses

1 A single high-energy beam would have a much higher energy **(1)** so it would destroy all cells with which it came into contact when fired at the body **(1)**, whereas many low-energy beams will not have sufficient photon energy by themselves to harm healthy cells **(1)**; however, when they are focused at a point, the energies of the individual beams add up to become a large energy that can kill the cancer tumour **(1)**.

2 Examples could include – toxic / poisonous **(1)**, too short or long a half-life **(1)**, do not emit gamma-rays / do emit alpha particles **(1)**.

47. Nuclear fission

1 Slow-moving neutrons **(1)** are absorbed by a nucleus **(1)**, which becomes unstable and splits **(1)**.

2 any four from: In a chain reaction each of the neutrons produced by fission can cause another nucleus to undergo fission **(1)** so the number of atoms undergoing fission increases very rapidly **(1)** and can cause an explosion **(1)**; in a controlled chain reaction some of the neutrons are absorbed by a different material **(1)** so only one neutron from each fission can cause another atom to fission **(1)**.

3 (a) so that they are easily absorbed by nuclei / do not miss the nuclei **(1)** causing the nucleus to become unstable **(1)** OR so the nucleus will become unstable **(1)** and split, releasing thermal energy **(1)**

(b) any two from: so that the extra neutrons are absorbed as only one neutron per fission needs to go on to produce further fission **(1)** because otherwise the reaction would become out of control **(1)** leading to an explosion **(1)**

48. Nuclear fusion

1 Two smaller nuclei **(1)** join together to form a more stable, heavier nucleus **(1)** and release energy as thermal energy **(1)**.

2 Fusion results in the joining of smaller nuclei **(1)** to form a nucleus with a slightly smaller mass; the left-over mass is converted to energy **(1)**. Fission results in the splitting of a larger nucleus to form more stable daughter nuclei of smaller mass **(1)**, with the small difference in mass being converted to energy **(1)**.

49. Extended response – Radioactivity

*Answer could include the following points **(6)**:

- Alpha particles / alpha source must be used.
- Alpha particles ionise the air, leading to the production of electrons and ions and allowing a current to flow.
- Alpha particles cannot reach the body because they are stopped by a few centimetres of air and so do not present a risk to people in the room.
- Beta particles and gamma-rays are much more penetrating and can reach the body and so would present a risk to people in the room.
- Beta particles and gamma-rays are dangerous if they reach the body because they can damage cells / cause cells to mutate, which could lead to illnesses such as cancer.

50. Scalars and vectors

1 (a) mass **(1)**

(b) electric field **(1)**

2 (a) 4 m/s **(1)**

(b) −4 m/s **(1)**

3 The satellite is travelling at a constant speed **(1)** but its direction is constantly changing as it is moving in a circle. **(1)** For the velocity to be constant, both speed and direction must not change. **(1)**

51. Interacting forces

1 Gravity is always an attractive force, whereas magnetism and the electrostatic force can be attractive or repulsive **(1)**.

2 Friction and drag always work to oppose motion / slow down a moving object **(1)**.

3 Contact forces are drag **(1)** and normal **(1)**. Non-contact force is the force of gravity acting on the ship **(1)**.

52. Gravity, weight and mass

1 (a) Mass is 76 kg; $W = m\,g = 76\,\text{kg} \times 3.75\,\text{N/kg}$ **(1)** = 285 **(1)** N **(1)**

(b) Mass is 76 kg; $W = m\,g = 76\,\text{kg} \times 26\,\text{N/kg}$ **(1)** = 1976 **(1)** N **(1)**

2 $g = W \div m$ **(1)** = 54 N ÷ 18 kg **(1)** = 3 N/kg **(1)**

53. Resultant forces

1 (a) two forces of 20 N acting parallel and upwards **(1)**

(b) two forces of 20 N acting anti-parallel **(1)**

2 It is accelerating **(1)** downwards **(1)**.

3 Any three from: Initial velocity direction will be upwards **(1)** but acceleration / resultant force will be downwards **(1)**, causing the ball to decelerate / eventually stop **(1)** before then accelerating back down to the ground **(1)**.

54. Work and energy

1 work done = $F\,s$ = 350 N × 30 m **(1)** = 10 500 **(1)** J **(1)**

2 $W = F\,s$ so $F = W \div s$ = 360 000 J ÷ 300 m **(1)** = 1200 **(1)** N **(1)**

3 Work done = gain in GPE = $m\,g\,h$ **(1)** = 25 kg × 10 N/kg × 40 m **(1)** = 10 000 J **(1)**

55. Forces and elasticity

1 (a) two equal forces **(1)** of tension acting in opposite directions **(1)**

(b) two equal forces **(1)** acting towards each other **(1)**

2 (a) any two suitable examples, e.g. springs **(1)**, elastic bands **(1)**, rubber **(1)**, skin **(1)**

(b) any two suitable examples, e.g. springs beyond the limit of proportionality **(1)**, putty **(1)**, Plasticine **(1)**, bread dough **(1)**, wet chewing gum **(1)**

3 Elastic deformation is when a material returns to its original shape on removal of the deforming force **(1)**, whereas inelastic deformation is when it does not return to its original shape on removal of the deforming force **(1)**.

56. Force and extension

1 (a) $F = k\,e$ = 30 N/m × 0.2 m **(1)** = 6 **(1)** N **(1)**

(b) work done = $\frac{1}{2}k\,e^2 = \frac{1}{2} \times 30\,\text{N/m} \times (0.2\,\text{m})^2$ **(1)** = 0.6 **(1)** J **(1)**

2 The greater the spring constant, the stiffer the spring **(1)** because a greater spring constant means that more force is needed **(1)** to provide the same extension compared with a spring of lower spring constant **(1)**.

3 The force applied takes the spring beyond its limit of proportionality **(1)** and so the material will remain permanently deformed **(1)** and not return to its original shape **(1)**.

57. Required practical – Force and extension

1 For a spring with a lower spring constant, the extension for the same weight will be greater **(1)** and the graph will be steeper **(1)**. For a spring with a higher spring constant, the extension for the same weight will be less **(1)** and the graph will be less steep **(1)**.

2 The spring would not return to its original length (**1**) when the weights are removed (**1**). The length of the spring would have increased (**1**) and the graph would not be a straight line at the top right (**1**).

3 Yes (**1**) because energy is still being stored and there is compression rather than an extension (**1**), so the size of the compression / length less than the original length would be used in the equations to determine the spring constant or the energy stored (**1**).

58. Moments

Clockwise and anticlockwise moments must balance (**1**).
$160\,\text{N} \times 1.5\,\text{m} = 200\,\text{N} \times d$ (**1**), so $d = 1.2\,\text{m}$ on the other side of the pivot (**1**)

59. Levers and gears

1 to increase the output force from the input force, such as when the car is starting to move or accelerate (**1**), to decrease output force with respect to the input force such as when the car has reached a high speed and wants to maintain a steady speed (**1**), and to change the direction of motion such as the use of gears to make the car reverse (**1**)

2 reference to higher output force than input force / force multiplier (**1**), reference to moments (**1**), reference to moment $= F\,d$ (**1**), reference to principle of moments / if clockwise and anticlockwise moments are the same, then output F is greater because output d (distance from load to the pivot) is smaller (**1**)

3 Gear wheels exert equal and opposite forces on each other (**1**) where their edges are in contact. The force on each gear wheel acts at right angles to the line to the centre of the wheel, and transmits a turning force (**1**). Levers apply a force at right angles to the pivot (**1**), so this can cause the body to rotate about the pivot (**1**).

60. Pressure

1 Pressure = force ÷ area = $750\,\text{N} \div 0.025\,\text{m}^2$ (**1**) = 30 000 (**1**) Pa (**1**)

2 $P = F \div A$, so $A = F \div P$ (**1**)
$600\,\text{N} \div 20\,000\,\text{Pa}$ (**1**) = 0.03 (**1**) m^2 (**1**)

3 Pressure depends on the force pressing down on the surface (**1**). As height increases, there is less air above you and the air becomes less dense (**1**). The force decreases and so pressure decreases (**1**).

61. Distance and displacement

1 The displacement from the pendulum's lowest point may be positive to the right (**1**) and negative to the left (**1**) and this displacement will constantly change in size and direction as it swings (**1**).

2 (a) If the starting point of the race is defined as zero displacement (**1**) then the athlete has returned to this point and his displacement is zero (**1**).

(b) The athlete has returned to the starting point (**1**) and then gone beyond the starting point (where displacement is zero) in the positive direction (**1**).

(c) The athlete may not have reached the finish line (**1**) and the displacement is in the opposite direction on the track (**1**) to the direction defined as having a positive displacement (**1**).

62. Speed and velocity

1 If a car is accelerating (**1**) then its speed is constantly changing, so its speed can be stated only at that instant (instantaneous speed) from the equation speed = distance ÷ time, or from the gradient of a distance–time graph at that instant (**1**). Average speed is the speed for the whole of a journey, regardless of whether the speed has been constant or has been constantly changing (**1**), and it is calculated using average speed = total distance travelled ÷ total time taken (**1**).

2 Distance = speed × time = $12\,\text{m/s} \times 60\,\text{s}$ (**1**) = 720 (**1**) m (**1**)

3 If the direction of a body is changing when it is moving at a constant speed, it is accelerating, because its direction is changing (**1**).

4 Time = distance ÷ speed = $800\,\text{m} \div 8\,\text{m/s}$ (**1**) = 100 (**1**) s (**1**)

63. Distance–time graphs

1 (a) Graph with distance on vertical axis and time on horizontal axis (**1**), appropriate scales on axes – 0–700 m on vertical axis and 0–700 s on horizontal axis (**1**), points (0, 0), (250, 400), (400, 400) and (700, 700) plotted (**1**) and joined with straight lines (**1**).

(b) Average speed = total distance ÷ total time = 700 m ÷ 700 s (**1**) = 1 (**1**) m/s (**1**)

2 (a) Person is stopped / stationary (**1**).

(b) Speed = change in distance ÷ change in time = $(60 - 40)\,\text{m} \div (40 - 20)\,\text{s}$ (**1**) = 20 m ÷ 20 s = 1 (**1**) m/s (**1**)

64. Velocity–time graphs

1 (a) horizontal line at a non-zero value on the y-axis (**1**)

(b) line of positive gradient (**1**)

(c) line of negative gradient (**1**)

(d) horizontal line along x-axis at $y = 0$ (**1**)

2 correct axes shown: velocity on y-axis and time on x-axis (**1**), horizontal line at 8 m/s shown for 12 s (**1**), positive linear gradient of 1.5 shown for the next 6 s (**1**), final velocity of 17 m/s shown after 18 s (**1**)

3 (a) change in velocity = 0 m/s, change in time = 10 s; acceleration = 0 m/s ÷ 10 s (**1**) = 0 m/s^2 (**1**)

(b) change in velocity = 10 m/s, change in time = 10 s; acceleration = 10 m/s ÷ 10 s (**1**) = 1 m/s^2 (**1**)

(c) change in velocity = 0 m/s, change in time = 20 s; acceleration = 0 m/s ÷ 20 s (**1**) = 0 m/s^2 (**1**)

(d) change in velocity = –10 m/s, change in time = 20 s; acceleration = –10 m/s ÷ 20 s (**1**) = –0.5 m/s^2 (**1**)

65. Equations of motion

1 $a = (8\,\text{m/s} - 2\,\text{m/s}) \div 5\,\text{s}$ (**1**) = 6 m/s ÷ 5 s = 1.2 (**1**) m/s^2 (**1**)

2 $v^2 - 0^2 = 2 \times 1.6\,\text{m/s}^2 \times 1800\,\text{m}$ (**1**) = 5760 (m/s)^2; $v = \sqrt{5760} = 75.9$ (**1**) m/s (**1**)

3 $v^2 - u^2 = 2as$: $v^2 - (20\,\text{m/s})^2 = 2 \times (-2\,\text{m/s}^2 \times 100\,\text{m})$ (**1**)
$v^2 = 400 - 400$ (**1**) = 0, so the car will stop in time (**1**)

66. Terminal velocity

1 sketch similar to that shown below with four stages: force positive but decreasing (**1**); force zero (**1**); force negative but increasing (**1**); force zero (**1**)

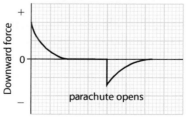

2 The diver reaches one terminal velocity only (**1**) due to the resistive forces exerted on her by the water (**1**), but the parachutist experiences two terminal velocities due to the air resistance when in free fall (**1**) and then later once the parachute has been opened (**1**). Students may also mention that the terminal velocity value for the diver may be much less than that of the parachutist due to the greater resistance when falling through water.

67. Newton's first law

1 balanced or equal and opposite **(1)** or no forces acting **(1)**

2 The forces acting on the moving body are in different / opposite directions **(1)** of different sizes **(1)** or a diagram drawn to show this. These forces could be antiparallel or even at an angle, such as at 90° to the initial movement. A change in direction will occur if the forces oppose the original motion or act in a way to change the direction.

3 diagrams showing:
   (a) equal forces of 100 N **(1)** and opposite **(1)** or no forces shown
   (b) equal forces of 100 N **(1)** and opposite forces **(1)** shown
   (c) two forces of 100 N **(1)** both acting to the left **(1)**

68. Newton's second law

1 $F = m\,a = 1.2\,\text{kg} \times 8\,\text{m/s}^2$ **(1)** $= 9.6$ **(1)** N **(1)**

2 $m = F \div a = 18.8\,\text{N} \div 0.8\,\text{m/s}^2$ **(1)** $= 23.5$ **(1)** kg **(1)**

3 $80\,\text{g} = 0.08\,\text{kg}$ **(1)**, $0.6\,\text{kN} = 600\,\text{N}$ **(1)**
   $a = F \div m = 600\,\text{N} \div 0.08\,\text{kg}$ **(1)** $= 7500$ **(1)** m/s^2 **(1)**

69. Required practical – Force, mass and acceleration

1 More accurate / repeat readings **(1)** can be taken with little or no human error **(1)** and calculations can be performed quickly by the data logger to provide speeds and accelerations, and so on **(1)**.

2 any four from: more accurate mass **(1)**, more accurate slope / gradient **(1)**, reduce friction **(1)**, more readings for mass **(1)**, repeat readings to determine the precision **(1)**

3 constant weight on weight stack throughout / other variables controlled **(1)**, change mass on glider by the same mass each time **(1)**, same starting point along track **(1)**, record enough values for change in velocity and change in times between two light gates **(1)**, repeat readings to determine the precision **(1)**

70. Newton's third law

1 If a body A exerts a force on body B **(1)** then body B will exert an equal and opposite force **(1)** on body A **(1)**.

2 The ball exerts a force on the goalkeeper's gloves **(1)** and the goalkeeper's gloves exert an equal and opposite force **(1)** on the ball **(1)**.

71. Stopping distance

1 Thinking distance increases by a factor of 4 **(1)**; braking distance increases by a factor of 16 **(1)**.

2 (a) kinetic energy $= \frac{1}{2} m v^2 = \frac{1}{2} \times 1250\,\text{kg} \times (12\,\text{m/s})^2$ **(1)** $= 90\,000$ **(1)** J **(1)**
   (b) kinetic energy lost = braking force × braking distance **(1)**, so $90\,000\,\text{J} = 1800\,\text{N} \times d$ **(1)** so $d = 90\,000 \div 1800$ **(1)** $= 50\,\text{m}$ **(1)**

72. Reaction time

1 (a) the time taken for a human to react to a stimulus **(1)**
   (b) 0.2 s **(1)** to 0.9 s **(1)**
   (c) any three of: tiredness **(1)**, alcohol **(1)**, drugs **(1)**, distractions **(1)**

2 Reaction time is proportional to the square root of the distance an object falls **(1)**. The square root of 4 is 2, so four times the distance means twice the reaction time **(1)**.

3 Distance is calculated using distance $= \frac{1}{2} g\, t^2$ **(1)**.
   When $t = 0.2\,\text{s}$, $s = \frac{1}{2} \times 9.8 \times (0.2)^2 = 0.196\,\text{m}$ **(1)**
   When $t = 0.9\,\text{s}$, $s = 3.969\,\text{m}$ **(1)**
   difference in distances $= 3.773\,\text{m}$ **(1)**

73. Extended response – Forces

*Answer could include the following points (**6**):
- Reaction times and thinking distance: as reaction time increases so does thinking distance. Reaction time is the time between seeing the hazard and applying a force to the brakes.
- Speed of car – affecting thinking and braking distance: more speed means a greater distance is covered when thinking and braking compared with a lower speed.
- Alcohol, drugs or tiredness affecting reaction times and thinking distance: both will increase if drivers are under the influence of these because they will be less alert.
- Condition of tyres: bald tyres mean greater braking distance because there will be less grip.
- Condition of road (icy or wet) resulting in less grip.
- Mass of car / number of passengers increases braking distance at a given speed due to greater inertial mass / constant force needed over a longer time to stop.

74. Waves

1 (a) amplitude **(1)**   wavelength **(1)**   for correct shape **(1)**

1(c) **(1)**

   (b) ← or → **(1)**
   (c) arrow shown above

2 (a) $T = 1/f = 1 \div 400\,\text{Hz}$ **(1)** $= 0.0025$ **(1)** s **(1)**
   (b) $f = 1/T = 1 \div 0.2\,\text{s}$ **(1)** $= 5$ **(1)** Hz **(1)**

75. Wave equation

1 $v = f \lambda = 14\,000\,\text{Hz} \times 0.024\,\text{m}$ **(1)** $= 336$ **(1)** m/s **(1)**

2 $f = v \div \lambda$, wave speed of a radio wave in air = speed of light, so $f = 300\,000\,000\,\text{m/s} \div 1200\,\text{m}$ **(1)** $= 250\,000$ **(1)** Hz **(1)** (or 250 kHz)

3 $\lambda = v \div f = (3 \times 10^8\,\text{m/s}) \div (2 \times 10^{20}\,\text{Hz})$ **(1)** $= 1.5 \times 10^{-12}$ **(1)** m **(1)**

76. Measuring wave velocity

1 $v = f \lambda = 4\,\text{Hz} \times 0.08\,\text{m}$ **(1)** $= 0.32$ **(1)** m/s **(1)**

2 Speed of sound in air is found by measuring a distance for the wave to travel and a time over which the distance is covered **(1)**. Having a large distance **(1)** and a large time **(1)** for these measurements, using equipment with a high degree of resolution / accuracy **(1)**, will lead to a low percentage of error.

77. Required practical – Waves in fluids

1 error in wavelength measured for the wave when distance being measured **(1)**, error in frequency value of the wave from generating source **(1)**, error when taking any time values with a stopwatch to find the wave speed **(1)**

2 Any three of: More wavelengths give a greater distance to measure **(1)** with a measuring device of a constant accuracy / resolution **(1)** so wavelength value will be more accurate because percentage error in value obtained will be less **(1)**; example given is a metre ruler being used to measure a wavelength of 10 cm with a 1-cm scale giving a 10% error, whereas measuring 10 wavelengths would mean a 1% error (or similar) **(1)**.

78. Waves and boundaries

1 They can be reflected, refracted, transmitted or absorbed. (**2 marks for all four, 1 mark for three correct**)

2 You get sunburnt by absorbing ultraviolet light (**1**) which is transmitted by the atmosphere and absorbed by skin (**1**), but is not transmitted by concrete walls so it cannot be absorbed by your skin when you are indoors (**1**).

3 (a) It stops infrared radiation reaching us (**1**), which could cause overheating / death (**1**).

   (b) Two of: It stops infrared radiation getting to us from space which could help us detect other objects in space (**1**); it may be useful when it is too cold to keep people or crops warm, etc. (**1**); it may have an impact on studies of the atmosphere or space, e.g. meteorology or climatology studies (**1**).

79. Required practical – Investigating refraction

1 its speed (**1**), its direction (**1**)

2 angles of refraction are less than their corresponding angles of incidence (**1**); angles of refraction are greater than the corresponding angles of refraction for those in the glass block (**1**)

3 (a) Frequency does not change (**1**) because the frequency is determined by the oscillating source that produces the wave and remains constant regardless of any change in speed or wavelength (**1**).

   (b) Wavelength decreases (**1**) because the wave speed decreases and the frequency remains constant (**1**).

80. Electromagnetic spectrum

1 (a) radio waves (**1**)

   (b) gamma-rays (**1**)

2 4×10^{-7} m: $f = v \div \lambda = 3 \times 10^8$ m/s $\div 4 \times 10^7$ m (**1**) = 7.5×10^{14} Hz (**1**); 7×10^{-7} m: $f = 3 \times 10^8$ m/s $\div 7 \times 10^{-7}$ m = 4.3×10^{14} Hz (**1**)

3 (a) frequency = $4 \times 10^{18} \div 60 = 6.7 \times 10^{16}$ Hz (**1**); $\lambda = v \div f = 3 \times 10^8$ m/s $\div 6.7 \times 10^{16}$ Hz (**1**) = 4.5×10^{-9} m (**1**)

   (b) X-rays (**1**)

81. Required practical – Infrared radiation

1 Curves will, in order of steepness, be silver (**1**), white (**1**), shiny black (**1**), dull black (**1**), because shiny is the worst emitter and dull black is the best emitter.

2 The rate (**1**) at which a hot body loses thermal energy (**1**) is directly related to its temperature (**1**) so a constant, fixed temperature is needed at the start in order that a fair test can be established for comparison (**1**).

82. Dangers and uses

1 X-rays are useful to doctors because they allow them to detect broken bones (**1**) but they can damage cells (**1**) which could cause them to mutate / lead to cancer (**1**).

2 Microwaves are absorbed by water molecules in the food (**1**) and their vibrations cause them to heat the food and cook it (**1**). Infrared cooks food by heating the surface of the food only (**1**) before the heat then conducts (**1**) into the food, cooking it over a longer period of time (**1**).

3 Ultraviolet waves can cause skin to age prematurely and increase the risk of skin cancer (**1**). X-rays and gamma-rays are ionising radiation that can cause the mutation of genes and cancer (**1**). Ultraviolet waves, X-rays and gamma-rays can have hazardous effects on human body tissue. The effects depend on the type of radiation and the size of the dose (**1**). Radiation dose (in sieverts) is a measure of the risk of harm resulting from an exposure of the body to the radiation (**1**).

83. Lenses

1 (a) real and virtual images (**1**)

   (b) virtual image only (**1**)

2 thickness of the lens (**1**), density of material / material it is made from (**1**)

3 Any two from: A real image can be produced on a screen but a virtual image cannot (**1**). A real image is usually upside down but a virtual image is usually upright (**1**). A virtual image can be produced by a concave and a convex lens, whereas a real image can be produced only by a convex lens (**1**).

84. Real and virtual images

1 (a) principal foci 4 cm either side of lens (**1**), object at correct position 12 cm from centre of lens (**1**), three rays drawn from top of object, one through the centre of the lens, one parallel to the principal axis to the lens, then going through the principal focus on the far side of the lens, and a third through the principal focus on the same side as the object to the lens, then parallel to the principal axis (**1**) with image shown in correct place (**1**)

   (b) smaller than the object (**1**), inverted / upside down (**1**), real (**1**)

   (c) magnification = 2.5 cm $\div$ 5 cm (**1**) = 0.5 (**1**)

85. Visible light

1 diffuse reflection (**1**)

2 Red light is let through the filter (transmitted) (**1**) and all of the other colours are absorbed (**1**).

3 You would see no colour (it would appear black) (**1**) because red would be let through the red filter but not through the green filter (**1**).

86. Black body radiation

1 The rate at which the body absorbs radiation (**1**) is greater than the rate at which it radiates / emits radiation (**1**).

2 B (**1**).

3 because dull black material is the best absorber of radiation (**1**) and the best emitter (**1**)

87. Extended response – Waves

*Answer could include the following points (**6**):

- Radio waves: including broadcasting, communications and satellite transmissions.
- Microwaves: including cooking, communications and satellite transmissions.
- Infrared: including cooking, thermal imaging, short-range communications, optical fibres, television remote controls and security systems.
- Visible light: including vision, photography and illumination.
- Ultraviolet: including security marking, fluorescent lamps, detecting forged bank notes and disinfecting water.
- X-rays: including observing the internal structure of objects, airport security scanners and medical X-rays.
- Gamma-rays: including sterilising food and medical equipment, and the detection of cancer and its treatment.

88. Magnets and magnetic fields

1 (a) similar to the diagram for the bar magnet (**1**) but with fewer field lines (**1**)

   (b) field lines shown with correct pattern (**1**); field lines closer together / more densely packed than for the weak magnet in part (a) (**1**)

2 The permanent magnet always induces (**1**) the opposite pole (**1**) next to its pole, causing it to attract (**1**).

89. Current and magnetism

1 similar to diagram on page 89 (**1**), but with the arrows in the opposite direction (**1**)

2 The current doubles so the field doubles (**1**) and the distance doubles so the field halves (**1**), so overall there is no change (**1**).

3 Increase the size of the current flowing (**1**), increase the number of turns of wire per metre on the coil (**1**), and insert a magnetic material as the core (**1**).

90. Extended response – Magnetism and electromagnetism

*Answer could include the following points (**6**):

- The closer a magnet is to an object, the stronger the magnetic field that it will experience, so the greater the mass it can attract.
- A greater electric current will cause the strength of the magnetic field around an electromagnet to be greater.
- More turns on the coil or a coiled wire rather than a straight wire increases the strength of the magnetic field from the electromagnetic field, so a greater mass can be picked up or attracted.
- Using a soft iron core will increase the strength of the magnetic field around a solenoid / electromagnet, so more mass can be attracted.
- Mention that certain materials in which magnetism can be induced will be attracted, whereas others will not – iron, cobalt, nickel, steel will be.
- Mention that certain materials that are themselves permanent magnets will be attracted based on their magnetic field strengths, even when no current flows through an electromagnet.

91. The Solar System

1 Neptune, Uranus, Saturn, Jupiter, Mars, Earth, Venus, Mercury (**2 marks: all 8; 1 or 2 incorrect: 1 mark**)

2 Greater distance (**1**) makes them dimmer (**1**); recent developments in telescopes allow these to be seen (**1**).

3 Stars and planets form from dust and gas (**1**) being pulled together by gravitational attraction (**1**), but stars are formed from much more mass / material than planets (**1**).

92. The life cycle of stars

1 (a) gravitational attraction of dust and gas (**1**), main-sequence star / hydrogen fusion (**1**), red giant / expansion after hydrogen burning phase (**1**), white dwarf / collapse (**1**)

(b) same as (a) until main sequence (**2**), followed by red supergiant and supernova explosion (**1**), followed by gravitational collapse to a neutron star for a massive star and to a black hole for a supermassive star (**1**)

2 This star radiates thermal energy as it loses heat (**1**) but gains temperature due to work being done on it by gravitational collapse, which raises its temperature (**1**).

3 Gravity pulls dust and gas together to form a nebula (**1**), leading eventually to fusion (**1**) with thermal pressure balancing this when a main-sequence star results from radiation pressure from fusion (**1**), until the thermal radiation pressure exceeds the pull of gravity at the end of the star's main-sequence life and it expands (**1**).

93. Satellites and orbits

1 Speed of a body in a circular orbit is constant (**1**) but velocity is changing because the direction of the body is constantly changing (**1**).

2 gravity (**1**)

3 (a) Any two from: both move in circular orbits (**1**) due to gravitational force (**1**) around bodies of greater mass (**1**).

(b) Any two from: artificial satellites are made by humans (**1**); used for GPS / weather / spying (**1**); they have different speeds (**1**); orbit circumferences are different (**1**); natural satellites or moons orbit planets, whereas artificial satellites orbit Earth (**1**)

94. Red-shift

1 the observed increase in wavelength of light (**1**) of a body that is moving away from the observer (**1**)

2 Observations of supernovae (**1**) suggest that distant galaxies are receding much faster than originally thought (**1**).

3 Red-shift shows that the Universe is expanding (**1**) because most distant galaxies are moving away from us / each other as space expands (**1**), but it does not provide evidence for the Big Bang actually happening; other evidence is needed to confirm this (**1**).

95. Extended response – Space physics

*Answer could include the following points (**6**):

- Low-mass stars expand to become red giants after the main sequence.
- Low-mass stars that become red giants then become white dwarfs.
- High-mass stars become red supergiants after they move off the main sequence.
- High-mass red supergiant stars undergo supernova explosions.
- Remnant cores of supernovae can become neutron stars (1.4–3 solar masses).
- Most massive stars become black holes (greater mass than 3 solar masses).

Physics Equation Sheet

In your exam, you will be provided with the following list of equations. Make sure you are clear which equations will be given to you in the exam. You will need to learn the equations that aren't on the equations list.

(final velocity)^2 – (initial velocity)^2 = 2 × acceleration × distance $v^2 - u^2 = 2\,a\,s$
elastic potential energy = 0.5 × spring constant × (extension)^2 $E_e = \frac{1}{2}\,k\,e^2$
change in thermal energy = mass × specific heat capacity × temperature change $\Delta E = m\,c\,\Delta\,\theta$
period = $\dfrac{1}{\text{frequency}}$
magnification = $\dfrac{\text{image height}}{\text{object height}}$
thermal energy for a change of state = mass × specific latent heat $E = m\,L$
For gases: pressure × volume = constant $p\,V = constant$

Your own notes

Your own notes

Your own notes

Your own notes

Published by Pearson Education Limited, 80 Strand, London, WC2R 0RL.

www.pearsonschoolsandfecolleges.co.uk

Text and illustrations © Pearson Education Limited 2018
Typeset, illustrated and produced by Phoenix Photosetting
Cover illustration by Miriam Sturdee

The right of Dr Mike O'Neill to be identified as author of this work has been asserted by him in accordance with the Copyright, Designs and Patents Act 1988.

First published 2018

24
10 9 8 7 6 5 4

British Library Cataloguing in Publication Data
A catalogue record for this book is available from the British Library

ISBN 978 1 292 13151 1

Printed by CPI Group (UK) Ltd, Croydon CR0 4YY

Acknowledgements
Content written by Penny Johnson and Steve Woolley is included in this revision guide.

Page 9, Trends in the world's energy use, graph includes data from BP Statistical Review of World Energy 2012 www.bp.com/statisticalreview; page 45, map is adapted from https://www.gov.uk/government/organisations/health-protection-agency, Radon Affected Areas in England and Wales – Health Protection Agency. Esri, HERE, DeLorme, FAO, NOAA, USGS. © Crown copyright. Contains public sector information licensed under the Open Government Licence (OGL) v3.0. http://www.nationalarchives.gov.uk/doc/open-government-licence/version/3/

Note from the publisher
Pearson has robust editorial processes, including answer and fact checks, to ensure the accuracy of the content in this publication, and every effort is made to ensure this publication is free of errors. We are, however, only human, and occasionally errors do occur. Pearson is not liable for any misunderstandings that arise as a result of errors in this publication, but it is our priority to ensure that the content is accurate. If you spot an error, please do contact us at resourcescorrections@pearson.com so we can make sure it is corrected.